D1267965

ACTOR AND ARCHITECT

Actor and Architect

by

TYRONE GUTHRIE

RICHARD SOUTHERN

SEAN KENNY

CHRISTOPHER STEVENS

HUGH HUNT

JOHN ENGLISH

edited by

STEPHEN JOSEPH

MANCHESTER UNIVERSITY PRESS

© 1964 MANCHESTER UNIVERSITY PRESS
Published by
the University of Manchester
THE UNIVERSITY PRESS
316–324 Oxford Road
Manchester 13

First published 1964
Reprinted 1969

GB SBN 7190 0011 4

Printed in Great Britain by
Butler & Tanner Ltd
Frome and London

CONTENTS

ILLUSTRATIONS

NOTES ON THE CONTRIBUTORS

GRENFELL BAINES

Is a partner in the firm of Building Design Partnership and is responsible for Stage II of the Humanities Building at Manchester University which will include the new University Theatre.

PERCY CORRY

Managing Director of the firm of Watts & Corry. He is an expert on theatre architecture and lighting.

W. A. DARLINGTON

He has been drama critic for the *Daily Telegraph* since 1920, and is also author of books and plays, including *Alf's Button*.

JOHN ENGLISH

A pioneer of the open stage in this country, he is a director of the Arena Theatre Company and is currently engaged in planning the theatre to be erected in connection with the Midlands Arts Centre in Birmingham.

SIR TYRONE GUTHRIE

Eminent British theatre director, his reputation and experience are world-wide. The Shakespeare Festival Theatre at Stratford, Ontario, which he designed, with Tanya Moiseiwitsch, and of which he was the first director, has been a notable and influential contribution to theatre architecture. Recently at Minneapolis the Tyrone Guthrie Theatre has been built, again to his requirements, and, since giving his talk at Theatre Week, he has directed the first season there.

HUGH HUNT

After considerable experience as a director in repertory theatres, culminating in work at the Abbey Theatre, Dublin, and the Bristol Old Vic, he was appointed director to the Old Vic in London. He then went, as director, to the Elizabethan Theatre Trust in Australia, and, soon after returning to England, became Professor of Drama in Manchester University.

STEPHEN JOSEPH

Is an expert on theatre in the round and has recently opened the Victoria Theatre, Stoke-on-Trent, which is the only permanent theatre in the round in the country. He is now a lecturer in the Manchester University Department of Drama.

SEAN KENNY

A well-known and original stage designer, whose contribution to such musicals as *Oliver* and *Blitz* have made him famous, he has also designed several notable productions for the Royal Shakespeare Company and the National Theatre. He is an architect and has radical views on theatre buildings for the future.

DAVID SCASE

Well known in Manchester as director of the Library Theatre, he has since gone to the Playhouse, Liverpool.

RICHARD SOUTHERN

One of the foremost scholars of theatre architecture, Dr Southern has published many books on this subject. He has been theatre consultant to several new theatres, including the one planned for Manchester University. He is lecturer in the Bristol University Department of Drama, and director of the University Theatre at Southampton.

CHRISTOPHER STEVENS

A partner in the firm of Powell and Moya, he was responsible for designing the Chichester Festival Theatre.

Preface

IN 1962 the Department of Drama in the University of Manchester held its second *Theatre Week*. The theme of *Actor and Architect* was chosen with the intention of exposing and exploring some of the issues connected with the building of new theatres and playhouses. These issues are of concern to the public. Not only are theatres public buildings in the sense that a live audience is part and parcel of a performance, but also (increasingly, these days) much of the money that pays for the buildings comes through the Arts Council or the local council from the ratepayer and the taxpayer. However, these issues are not often discussed in public by experts, and most people simply do not know that the generally accepted concept of a theatre is now being held in question. Further, the emphasis of the question itself is continually shifting. Here are issues on which it is impossible to be dogmatic, but where it is often necessary to overstate the case in order to make clear a novel standpoint. The talks given during *Theatre Week* were therefore highly informal. The atmosphere was of adventure. Lecturers' notes did not commonly appear on the lectern. The talks seemed mostly to be spontaneous and they were given by people who seemed only just to have left the projects under discussion, which would be taken up again as soon as the immediate discussions were over, with everyone, possibly, a bit clearer in his mind about the practical job in hand. No original research was done and no special studies were undertaken.

The talks given in *Theatre Week* form the main part of this book; but at the time there were also performances of plays which contributed more or less to the week's theme. *Ralph Roister Doister* was presented as though on a booth stage (in the limiting space of the Arthur Worthington Hall); a performance of *The Bacchae* in the Whitworth Hall explored the field of theatre in the round; a welcome visit from the Drama Department of Bristol University gave an example of the techniques of staging Japanese Noh plays (again suffering from confinement in the Arthur Worthington Hall); and finally the University Stage

Society production of *Mother Courage* made good use of the picture-frame stage. In addition to these performances an exhibition of plans, drawings and photographs illustrated the week's theme by showing how, in its long evolution, the theatre has tried, in different ways, to serve the needs of actors and audiences.

All this may seem a strange way of employing the talents of a department in a university. Surely if drama is to justify itself as an academic discipline it must become studious, serious, specialized, remote, and (at least to the general public) incomprehensible? Possibly. But certainly not all the time. Perhaps a university should sometimes participate in the life of its neighbourhood; and what better meeting ground than theatre? But more than that, and more important than merely letting the public in on a few tricks of the theatrical building trade, is the fact that the public must be the eventual arbiter of taste in all matters related to the theatre. It is therefore important that the public should know about this new movement in theatre building. How can people ever choose new forms of theatre if they have neither seen nor heard of them? They have a right to information at least; and to begin an acquaintance with new ideas is a necessary step towards knowledge and experience.

Two distinct developments in theatre emerged with the beginning of the second half of the twentieth century. Firstly, in the 1950s a new generation of playwrights forced freshness into a drama whose conventions had grown stale. The change, fairly sudden and precise, was recognized and welcomed almost immediately. The new playwrights—such as Osborne, Pinter and Wesker—became well known not only in the theatre but also in the world of letters and in public affairs. The other development was a growing interest in new forms of theatre. This movement had several (and some uncertain) origins. Its beginning was hardly recognized and scarcely welcomed. Even when a clear pattern of change had become apparent, its activities remained more a matter of theoretical discussion than the business of actual building. In discussion, even, its intentions were misunderstood; and its terminology, tangled in argument, added to the confusion.

The first movement has been, of course, much written about.

The plays themselves are published and many books deal with the various writers and their significance. But not only have few theatres been built, little has been written about the new forms of theatre; and architects' drawings are never easily available to the public. This is not surprising. It is generally assumed that new plays are important to the theatre, while new buildings are not; after all, it is supposed, a play can be done anywhere. But the new plays and new playwrights have been little more than a nine days' wonder. In spite of all the persuasive criticism, the plays have not attracted big new audiences to the theatre, which, in general, still seems to be ailing. I suggest that one good reason can be found in our old and inadequate theatres. The persistence of the Victorian playhouse (which was solidly built) has been a root cause of both the delay preceding our new movement in playwriting and its short duration. The fresh vision of the young writers has been clouded over in the old-fashioned theatres; it has been a matter of putting new wine into old bottles. There is no real rivalry between the demands of writers and those of architects. New plays are indeed important, and a healthy theatre will surely always have them at hand. It is only an impoverished theatre, like our own, that has to give a special welcome to a new group of playwrights. In our case the theatre has been, and still is, deprived of suitable buildings in which to present plays. The conclusion is clear. To maintain a steady supply of new plays we must also continually build new theatres.

Although the importance of plays is commonly recognized and the importance of buildings is denied, this second movement, provided it can eventually achieve recognition, is likely to have the more profound effect on our drama. If we can sort out the tangle of words and ideas, we may find through our new buildings a way of establishing the live theatre, with its ever new dramatists, as a valid activity in our own society; if not, it seems likely that the drama, with new waves of writers or without, will do no better than remain a cliquish activity for relatively few people. Faced with these alternatives, a choice should not be difficult; but many devotees of theatre would state the case differently—as between a long and stable tradition on the one hand and, on the other, a stupid and potentially destructive unorthodoxy. The case for new theatres and new theatre forms is therefore worth pleading. This sets the scene, as it were, for a complicated argument.

It is appropriate, perhaps, to conduct the argument, in this book as in *Theatre Week,* with several different characters. Most of the arguments have a bias towards accepting the new movement in theatre design as helpful. But there is no agreement on the path to be followed. The idea of a path suggests something narrow. The issues are too complicated for that. There cannot be one solution. Here is the outline, rather, of a whole road system.

As editor I am grateful to the contributors who have helped me adapt their informal talks for the purposes of this book. I am grateful to Richard Southern and Sean Kenny, each of whom has illustrated his own contribution; to the Director of the Musei Civici, Venice, for permission to reproduce the drawings of the Teatro Olimpico; to the Superintendent of the Uffizi Galleries at Florence for permission to reproduce the drawings of the Teatro all'antiqua at Sabbioneta; to the *Architects' Journal* for permission to reproduce the photograph of the Festival Theatre at Chichester; to Powell and Moya for permission to reproduce the drawing of the Festival Theatre at Chichester.

I prepared this book while holding the fellowship in the Department of Drama at the University of Manchester; for the fellowship I am very grateful to the Granada Television Company who initiated it—as they did, in fact, the department itself.

STEPHEN JOSEPH

1964

1
Introduction

STEPHEN JOSEPH

A THEATRE building is usually made up of a large number of rooms. Some of them, such as refreshment rooms and cloakrooms, are designed to look after the needs of the audience before they go into the auditorium. Some of them, such as dressing-rooms and wardrobe rooms, cater for the needs of actors before they go on to the stage. Others, including offices and workshops, provide working spaces for staff and technicians. Important as these rooms are, obviously the most vital spaces in a theatre are the stage and auditorium. It is these spaces that give the main traits of character to the building that we call a theatre. They are therefore the main subjects of controversy in discussion on new forms of theatre.

For most people the idea of a theatre derives from their experience of the picture-frame or proscenium stage. It is the common form of theatre in this country, throughout Europe and (though to a lesser extent) in America and the Commonwealth. It is widespread because it has had a long history. Most people assume that it is the only possible form of theatre for us. They regard other forms, if they have come across them at all, as exotic or antique, and irrelevant. This attitude arises from simple ignorance of facts. Not only is the picture-frame stage a manifestation of fashion and, like all fashionable things, liable to change, but its suitability for use as a playhouse is particularly open to question. There are many valid forms of stage which have been (and still are) successfully used for playhouses, and we shall be concerned with these throughout this book. But first it may be as well to say a little about the history of the picture-frame stage.

The enquiry may be restricted to Europe, since the picture-

1

frame stage has a complete and continuous history here. The first building with a permanent picture-frame stage can be taken as the Teatro Farnese in Parma, built by Aleotti and completed in 1618. The antecedents of the Teatro Farnese help to explain its form. Throughout Europe during the renaissance courtly and kingly entertainments were conducted on an impressive scale. Jousts and triumphs, feasts and balls, processions and masques, all gave opportunities for ostentation and display. Where these shows spilled over into the field of drama they were not, of course, biased towards any particular form of theatre. But one latent element pointed towards the picture-frame stage—the need to focus display towards a particular person or group of persons (the king, the duke, the newly married couple and so on). There seems to have been no conscious striving to achieve such a focus through architectural form. It came as an accidental benefit with other developments. Two main factors actively shaped the theatre. A renewed interest in classical art and architecture led back to Roman and Greek drama. This aspect of the renaissance is too well known to need careful exposition here, but it is worth recalling that the first printing in Rome of Vitruvius' work on architecture (including the architecture of ancient theatres) was published in 1486; an illustrated edition was published in Venice in 1511. In the middle of the sixteenth century came Serlio's treatise on perspective, Barbaro's illustrated edition of Vitruvius, and several attempts to rehabilitate the classical Roman theatre. Such attempts were often misguided, and they had, anyhow, to meet an entirely fresh social situation; the renaissance theatres were on a far smaller scale, they catered for aristocrats rather than the mob and they were destined for new entertainments. The Teatro Olimpico, referred to by Dr Southern on page 54, remains the nearest to a purely classical reconstruction. It was built for the Academy at Vicenza, and its purpose was primarily academic. The architect, Palladio, laid down the plan slightly differently from the accepted idea of an ancient Roman theatre—because his site was the wrong shape; thus do actual circumstances often tend to modify an ideal. Palladio died before the building was complete, and Scamozzi took over the work. Scamozzi is usually credited with the fine perspectives that fill the archways in the walls of the stage. The theatre

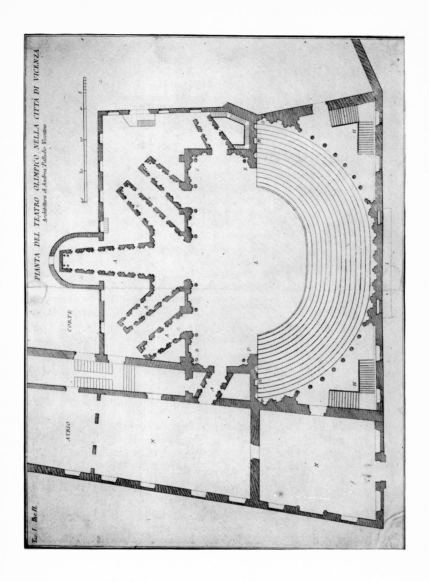

Tav. I Par. II.   PIANTA DEL TEATRO OLIMPICO NELLA CITTÀ DI VICENZA

Architettura di Andrea Palladio Vicentino

PLATE I
Plan of the
Teatro
Olimpico
at
Vicenza

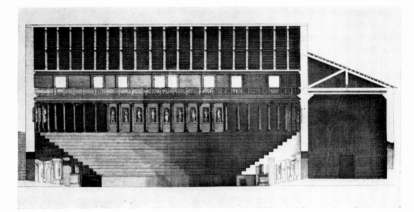

PLATE II. Sections of the Teatro Olimpico at Vicenza

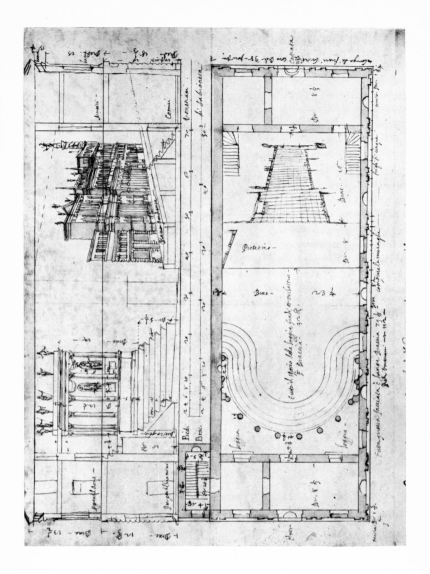

PLATE III
Plan and
section of the
Teatro
all'Antiqua
at
Sabbioneta

opened in 1585 with a performance of an opera, *Oedipus Rex*; the subject was classical and the operatic form itself had been devised in the mistaken belief that this was how the ancient Roman and Greek plays must have been performed. The Teatro Olimpico had an architectural background, intended to provide a permanent setting for any play (or opera) likely to be done there. But not much allowance was made for renaissance ostentation on the stage.

Scamozzi built another theatre, which is not, perhaps, of great importance except in the differences between the two. In the *teatro all'antiqua* at Sabbioneta he abandoned any attempt to repeat the Roman theatre plan. The main walls form a rectangle, externally nearly three times as long as it is wide. At either end a small space is allocated to foyer and to dressing-rooms. The stage is approximately square; at the front about one-third of it is flat and the remaining two-thirds slope steeply upwards, in the manner of the perspectives at the Teatro Olimpico. Here, though, there are no archways; the flat area simply gives on to the perspective. The audience is arranged on two levels. An upper level forms a ducal enclosure; it is fronted by Palladian pillars, sweeping in a semi-circle from wall to wall of the theatre. This is a brilliant development of the Olimpico plan, made feasible by the altogether smaller scale of the theatre at Sabbioneta, which has, all the same, a proportionately greater length. In front of the pillared gallery, semi-circular rows of benches step steeply down to the auditorium floor. But the ends of the semi-circular rows are curved back to meet the side walls of the theatre. There is now an extraordinary mixture of focal points. The semi-circular benches focus on to a large arena in the middle of the auditorium. The arena extends beyond the semi-circles to include a floor space that is the full width of the room, for a depth greater than the depth of the flat part of the stage. Both the arena and the stage are equally within the focus of viewing from the ducal gallery. Of course, the vanishing point of the perspective vista has its horizon line at eye-level from the gallery. There are thus a number of performance areas, shifting between arena and stage.

The theatre at Sabbioneta has been damaged, and, at one time or another, carelessly restored. However, it is possible to notice two further important features. Firstly, the whole theatre was a magnificent mixture of architecture, sculpture, and painting which invited the addition of living people. Sculptured pillars and balustrades merged into painted ones; real perspectives, false perspectives and painted perspectives carried on the structural and decorative scheme without a break. Real people in the audience and on the stage would meet life-size statues and life-size paintings on the walls—a musician here, a spectator there. This brazen mixture of art and life reflects a careless vigour and skill to be found in many late renaissance buildings; there are tantalizing examples in the nearby ducal palace where perspectives painted on the walls give many fascinating *trompe l'œil* effects. It is easy to understand that the stage did not need a picture frame. As far as can be judged from the present state of the building the ceiling extended over the whole auditorium. But, probably, it did not cover the stage. More likely, over the whole stage clouds and sky-borders were suspended, and over the flat part of the stage there was machinery which could move the clouds and, more importantly, let in actors—on sky-borne chariots, eagles, and planets. This is surmise. Certainly such effects were already available. Somewhere the crucial combination was made; the renaissance love of courtly ostentation meets the concern with classical theatre, and finally sparks off a new invention—the theatre with movable scenery. And with movable scenery comes machinery to achieve better and better effects; and with machinery, a masking framework to conceal the labour and reveal the spectacle.

Aleotti's theatre at Parma, altogether bigger than Scamozzi's at Sabbioneta, retains the ducal gallery. The semi-circles of benches straighten out at their open ends and form a vast arena (which could be flooded for water-shows). They seem to put more emphasis on the arena than on the stage. But the stage is marked out by a magnificent frame. Behind the frame, a gently sloping stage was designed for moving wings and other scenic machinery. It is open to doubt whether actors were ever intended to perform on the stage, except as part of the spectacle (when they may have descended in the usual clouds and other planetary conveyances). Besides, the theatre was not built for plays. It was built for shows; particularly opera. The large arena suggests that dancing and courtly masking were certainly major considerations.

The picture-frame stage was invented by people highly skilled in painting, sculpture and architecture, to provide the spectacular entertainment of moving pictures. During the following centuries, the development of this form of theatre was affected by demands from all over Europe—of opera in Italy, ballet in France (and later in Russia), melodrama in Germany and pantomime in England. But it remained a place for moving pictures. Play-actors got involved in spite of themselves. Once behind the frame actors could be heard less easily, and they ceased to share the same room as the audience. They were diminished. Actors from Cibber onwards were quick to notice this. And it was not until a stable pattern of theatre building had become established that actors ceased to consider the possibility of any further change or alternative. In England the picture-frame theatre reached something like a final pattern at the end of the nineteenth century. Most of our existing theatres date back to this era. In each building the fundamental characteristic has remained a division into two rooms, one containing the audience, the other containing the stage and stage machinery. The actual arrangement of seating has varied during the centuries of development, and has never become entirely standardized, particularly in the number of seating levels (circles, galleries and so on). Stage machinery changed with the industrial revolution, and scene-shifting techniques have come to rely not only on wing-space for movable flats but also on an overhead tower for flying-out cloths, etc. Elevators, trucks and revolving stages have been used from time to time but have never become generally accepted; they make little difference to the structure of the stage room. Only one entirely new device has been added to the picture-frame stage—electricity; and even this in the main serves only to replace the more cumbersome light of gas and, earlier still, candles and oil lamps. Centuries of development have led to a measure of perfection, but the perfection belongs to the era which produced it and the entertainments which it accommodated.

Another important detail in the story of the picture-frame stage is its relationship to photography. There is far too much to be said on this subject for full description here. But there is an early link between the study of perspective images in the *camera obscura* and perspective scenery. The *camera obscura*, from the renaissance onwards, was commonly used by artists, particularly for topographical drawing. A painting on framed canvas can depict all that is observed in the camera, except movement. Painted scenery can supply the movement. Garrick's great scenic artist, de Loutherbourg, invented the eidophusikon, an entertainment of moving pictures with sound effects. Late in the eighteenth century a person was born who admirably summarizes, in his life's work, the different elements in this connection. As a young man he wanted to be a painter; he was apprenticed first to an architect then to a scene designer. He spent half a dozen years as an assistant to a famous painter of 'panoramas', then became famous for realistic and spectacular scenery in the theatre. He made particularly effective use of lighting. In the 1820s he invented the tremendously popular Diorama, and almost immediately began work on the researches that were to lead to his most famous achievement, to fix the images of the *camera obscura*. This was, of course, Daguerre. Years later, the movie camera provided the logical conclusion. It is no coincidence that the theatre, with a picture frame, for showing moving pictures, should turn out to be a ready-made cinema. It is a bit more difficult to accept the fact that the main function of the picture-frame stage has now been entirely taken over by the film industry. Cinema architecture has made its own advances to keep pace with the wide screen, leaving the theatre proudly in possession of the old picture frame, which often seems to me no more than a pathetic left-over of little importance in modern entertainment and still less in modern life.

In my opinion, the picture-frame stage, no matter how glorious its past, has never had much connection with the drama, and it is now an incubus which is suffocating live entertainment. I may be mistaken in my view, but certainly an unkind comment or two seem necessary if only to shake people out of their lethargic acceptance of the traditional theatre structure. We must, of course, acknowledge that the picture-frame stage has played an important part in the story of the drama, and many fine theatres have been built in this form. It would be wrong to condemn them on every score. Old buildings of any sort contribute usefully to our whole way of life. They are often objects of unique beauty. But, on this account, to ignore modern forms is simply to reject life and to sink into pessimism. New architectural forms now demand our attention.

It is not correct to suggest, in attack or defence, that the picture-frame stage is incapable of further development. Its evolution could be expected to continue in the face of social and artistic pressures, as it has in fact developed recently in Germany and the United States. As far as this country is concerned there seem to be three directions which architects of the picture-frame stage might immediately explore. Firstly, size; the eighteenth-century demand for bigger and bigger theatres seems to have landed us with buildings too big for most modern plays. An example of increasing accommodation can be got nicely from the Theatre Royal in Drury Lane. The first theatre of 1663 held about 700 people; the second, built by Wren, 2,000. The third, Holland's theatre, opened in 1794 and accommodated 3,611. The fourth theatre, designed by Wyatt and opened in 1812, had a capacity of 3,060. This theatre, remodelled, is the present one. It now accommodates 2,226 people. A modern playhouse would be more likely to approach the first figure, 700, rather than any other. Bigger theatres may be required for some purposes, but there is no urgent need to build them; they already exist.

Another way in which the picture-frame stage might develop is in its scene-changing techniques. The grid tower provides for flying cloths; it can be used for flats and more solid scenery. However, as scenery for plays is increasingly a matter of sets of flats and three-dimensional units, the alternative method of using truck stages has much to recommend it. Trucks demand greater wing and back-stage space, but no grid tower. Architectural plan and elevation will alter accordingly. The grid tower is a very expensive structure; but wing-space for trucks demands more site area. Siting and capital expenditure are important factors. Finally, a third and purely technical consideration is likely to influence the design of picture-frame stages, front-of-house lighting. In the days when stage lighting involved naked flames it was expedient to try to keep stage lighting within the stage area. The brightness and control (and relative safety) that came with modern spotlights allow them to be placed in a variety of positions. It is possible to consider placing them where they may best achieve their main purposes, of enabling the audience to see the actors, and giving an added device to help the actors in performance. If it seems incongruous to state simple facts about electricity in the middle of the twentieth century, the explanation is that most of our theatres were built for stage lighting that is now no longer used, and they simply cannot accommodate the new lighting techniques. The spotlights are simply not in the right places. Merely to put up a new building does not necessarily mean that this will be remedied. Indeed, we tend to do what has always been done, repeating mistakes and all. For example the new Royalty Theatre, built in 1960, had an entirely inadequate lighting system, designed on traditional and out-of-date principles; the instruments themselves were new enough but, amongst other details, the front-of-house spotlights were in the wrong places and the design of the auditorium precluded their being better sited. This was a major factor in the failure of the theatre, which became a cinema within a year of opening.

It is conceivable that development might lead the picture-frame stage bit by bit to another form. With the addition of a forestage and the widening of the proscenium opening, an approach would be made towards a pictorial open stage. Something of the sort can be seen in the U.S.A., particularly in James Hull Miller's theatres—the Waco Civic Theatre, the Midland Community Theatre, Western Springs and others. Richard Leacroft has claimed that 'variations on this form of theatre could permit the widest range of theatrical expression using twentieth-century scenic methods, and moreover it has the added, and extremely important, advantage of providing them in a more economical manner'.[1]

But, whatever may be happening in the United States, there is a resistance to developing the picture-frame stage in this country. In fact the very elements of tradition and antiquity are among the strongest rallying points for theatre people. The preservation of old theatres not only commands more support than the building of new ones, but also ensures that new ones

[1] 'Actor and Audience' by Richard Leacroft, AADIPL (HONS.), MSIA(A), *RIBA Journal*, April and May 1963.

shall be built just like the old. Strangely enough, though, the decorative finishes may be contemporary while the stage area itself must remain old-fashioned, as at the Belgrade in Coventry.

II

Meanwhile alternative forms of theatre have also been proposed, and some have actually been built. The Mermaid Theatre and the Chichester Festival Theatre are examples of end-stage and open-stage theatres; the New Nottingham Playhouse is an adaptable theatre; and there is much talk about theatre in the round.

Where do these new forms spring from, and why are they now challenging the monopoly of the picture-frame stage? It is not easy to separate the strands of theory without tangling the cord of argument; but, roughly speaking, our ideas for new forms of theatre derive from four sources. Firstly, within the history of the theatre itself there can be found many different forms; Poel and others who tried to recapture the conditions of Shakespearian presentation have led us, through such buildings as the Maddermarket, indirectly to the Chichester Festival Theatre. It is important to recognize that the Elizabethan theatre movement has been very strong in the U.S.A., where several universities have built replicas, as accurately as modern scholarship permits, of Shakespeare's Globe Theatre; nothing comparable has so far been done in this country, but we have, as yet, only two university drama departments. Chichester was inspired directly by Stratford, Ontario. Producers such as Reinhardt, in a turbulent search for excitement, made use of medieval staging conventions. Much of the modern theory of theatre in the round is based on medieval practices. The oriental theatre has contributed features to some American stages and might be traced as an element in the design of the Vieux Colombier, in Paris, and thus to the Mermaid, though the strongest historical influence on the Mermaid is clearly the Elizabethan theatre (and the actual story of the Mermaid is of an Elizabethan stage idea transformed into a wholly modern theatre). Many other historical and exotic imitations have been incorporated into modern ideas and modern buildings.

A second source of new theatre forms has been the inspiration and the rivalry of the cinema. At times the theatre has striven to outdo the cinema; in realism and spectacle the cinema from the start seized the initiative from the theatre, but it has still not entirely triumphed. One of the reasons for the present appeal of small theatres is the increased realism of performance which they allow. And the present demand, on the other hand, for bigger and better stage machinery shows a desire to bring back to the theatre its supremacy in the spectacular field. Productions such as *Blitz* leave no doubt that spectacle in the theatre is still a potent means of entertainment. The cinema may have usurped some of the theatre's functions but certainly not all. The idea behind the phrase *live theatre* indicates exactly where the cinema cannot compete, and where therefore the theatre may find its greatest appeal—in the living actor. This leads us, almost inevitably, towards small theatres, or at least theatres where every member of the audience can see and hear the actors clearly, one of the most important issues in Sir Tyrone Guthrie's argument for an open stage.

Thirdly there are a number of loosely associated social and economic forces at work. During the war many theatres were destroyed; further, the value of theatre sites has been among the reasons for the closure of many theatres; a new picture-frame theatre is an expensive item, too expensive for private patrons, building speculators or civic authorities to embark on readily. And we have no established pattern of civic or state subsidy as they have, for instance, in Germany. The pressure of economy has forced some people to look at new forms of theatre which may be, seat for seat, comparatively cheaper to build. Even more important, perhaps, though far less clearly defined, is the inescapable fact that theatres are themselves an expression of their times; the gilt and plush of the Victorian theatre have now lost their original meaning and must obviously be replaced; and so, though perhaps less obviously, must the staging techniques too. Is there something more appropriate to our own day in the permanent architectural setting proposed, but never entirely used, both at the Mermaid and at Chichester, or in no setting at all (as for theatre in the round)? A theoretical answer is not good enough. The theatres themselves must eventually provide the real answer. Though it is interesting to note that an existentialist interpretation of central staging has already been suggested by Professor Kernodle.[1]

Finally, schools and colleges have begun to take an increasing interest in drama, both for its own sake and for its intrinsic values as an educational device. This has meant that various forms of theatre have begun to be studied; informal actor/audience relationships have been explored; and, owing to the inadequacy of most school halls, education authorities have looked for a solution to their particular problems where related problems in the professional theatre are also being solved. Teachers' training colleges have already pioneered the idea of the shell structure in which almost any form of stage can easily be erected. Such theatres can be seen, for instance, at St Mary's, Twickenham, and the James Graham College, Leeds. A drama school is a special case, but the influence of the new adaptable theatre at LAMDA is likely to be colossal.

It would be wrong to make even a brief survey of the origins of our current interest in new forms of theatre without saying more about our theatrical relationships with Europe and America. Most of our immediate exchange is confined to successful plays, the most convenient commodity for business men to handle. As far as the architecture of theatres is concerned, this country is almost in isolation. We have heard about the wonderful new theatres in Germany and we may even have seen a few of them. But as already mentioned, the Germans have a long tradition of subsidy which we have not. Many people notice besides that, in spite of their new theatres, they have not produced a wave of new writers to rival ours. Not only can we not afford to build splendid new theatres, but perhaps after all we don't really need them; writers and actors can do their work under the most appalling conditions, which may even, apparently, be more encouraging to them. This is a limited argument. The Germans are mainly interested in opera and build their theatres for huge opera companies. Our theatres are usually proposed as playhouses. They don't get playwrights, perhaps, and they don't need them—but we don't get playhouses and we need them desperately. I suspect our loss is nothing to be proud of. The United States is further away and,

[1] 'The Open Stage: Elizabethan or Existentialist' by George R. Kernodle, in *Shakespeare Survey*, 12, Cambridge, 1959.

in the main, we are only aware that Broadway is even more old-fashioned and commercialized than our own West-End. A few people may know of the work done by hundreds of university drama departments, of small community theatres, and of avowedly experimental theatres; they are too numerous to mention, and they include almost every sort of theatre. We ignore the fact that the so-called new forms of theatre have already been through tests of experience abroad.

It must also be noted that much the same blindness seems to apply to conventional picture-frame theatres, which we build badly in spite of good examples everywhere, even in our own country. It is extraordinary that a country that boasts, say, the Drury Lane Theatre and the Glyndebourne Opera House, should build, for example, the Prince Charles Theatre or the Ashcroft, Croydon. These last two theatres are conventional and modern, yet both suffer from technical inadequacies. They are inefficient. Such comment may seem arbitrary since, after all, they are very different and surely they cannot be dismissed with the same criticism. It may be worth making more detailed examination of them, but obviously a thorough examination would be out of place here, and certainly many good points in favour of each building must be taken for granted. The main inadequacy of the Prince Charles is merely one of space. As a playhouse it has too little wing space and back-stage space; it has no overhead flying space. It serves very well for small-scale revues and recitals, but as a playhouse it is entirely inadequate; unfortunately it has been accepted uncritically by people who may now wish to imitate it. The Ashcroft Theatre is an altogether more ambitious affair and needs to be taken more seriously. The division of the auditorium into two levels, with a balcony at the back of the theatre, means that people in the balcony feel very remote from the stage, even though the theatre holds no more than 750 people. The proscenium opening is emphasized by two side-towers, and these increase the separation of actors from audience. It is, of course, a matter of opinion how close or distant actors should be from their audience, but this particular example seems to be a very uncomfortable arrangement. Back stage there is poor circulation; the dressing-rooms are on upper floors and the staircases are shared with the public—which may be audiences from other entertainments in the main hall (boxing, concerts and meetings are held there). Mistakes like these need not be made. Whatever theatre is being built, traditional picture-frame or new forms of open stage, large or small, a high degree of efficiency should be possible, but is seldom achieved. A recent and notable exception is the workable and delightful little Civic Theatre at Hampstead, which only wants more storage space to make it excellent of its kind.

III

In the face of so many old theatres, and so much inefficiency in new ones, it is easy to be pushed to a deterministic conclusion: perhaps we are simply living in an age that cannot build theatres (but can beget playwrights). This is a lame conclusion; more likely we have been so complacent that we have not really asked ourselves the basic questions, starting with the simple one, 'What is a theatre for?' I suggest that that question must be answered in terms of actors and audience. This is where Sarcey begins.[1] A theatre is a place where a relatively large number of people assemble to see and hear actors performing. (It is this bald description, incidentally, that suggests the title *Actor and Architect* for a study of theatre design.) But the fact is that in most of our theatres it is not possible for each member of the audience to see and hear the actors. Sometimes the theatre is simply too big. More often the acoustics or the sight-lines are badly arranged. They may have been sacrificed to other requirements, and the extent of the sacrifice is the extent to which they have ceased to be theatres and have become buildings dedicated to whatever the preferred requirement is. But more commonly there is no positive conflict. Theatres are built badly from carelessness or ignorance, arising often enough from copying the superficial outlines of existing buildings; the basic question has never been asked. Obviously this attitude leads to the rejection of new forms of theatre; they do not resemble the superficial outlines of existing buildings and their ability to serve the essential functions of theatre is therefore not considered.

Such an attitude does not entirely account for our reluctance

[1] Francisque Sarcey, *Essais d'une Esthétique de théâtre,* Paris 1876.

to accept new forms of theatre. A more important consideration is the virtual monopoly of the one form, propped up by our pragmatic approach to the arts. We accept what is there without question. We have many picture-frame stages and very few other forms. This may argue that people prefer the picture-frame; though choice can hardly be exercised where there is so little variety. There is a respectable ancestry to the attitude that whatever is, is right. There are, of course, very powerful objections to new forms of stage; when there is so little theatre building at least let us build in a pattern that has served for so long; the fact that we build new picture-frame stages badly indicates that we shall build new forms even worse; and, let us be practical, we know very little about the new forms (will the audiences accept them, can the actors act in them, where can we find the plays for them?) so surely it is sensible to wait and see. In other words, it is folly to build new forms of theatre until new forms of theatre have been built. Reduced to mockery this is absurd enough, but it is a dominant consideration in councils where civic theatres are now being discussed in all seriousness. As a nation we tend to be conservative; we are particularly cautious in the arts; and we trust our own experience without being inclined to submit to experiment. We like the *status quo* and we mistrust theorists who propose new ideas. In fact, there are so many arguments against the new forms of theatre that only a very strong-minded person or an extremist is likely to take the weaker side. Thus a further objection to the new forms of theatre is that their protagonists are intellectuals or eccentrics, that they know nothing about the theatre, or that they in fact wish to destroy it; they are on no account to be taken seriously. But few of the reasons for not accepting the new forms of theatre actually arise from the forms themselves, and most opponents have had little chance even to see the new forms they so readily condemn.

This is not the place in which to list the particular characteristics and advantages of each form of stage, and it is doubtful if any one person has, at present, the experience and the detachment to do so with impartiality. Most of the contributors to this book have a preference, and advocate it more or less. My own preference will be clear enough, and in my contribution to the Brains Trust I have stated it categorically. I have worked in many different forms of theatre and have liked them all. If I now prefer theatre in the round it may be simply because I have, for ten years, explored this particular form. It is now a controversial subject and nearly everyone who discusses theatre architecture has something to say about it. To give theatre in the round preferential treatment here is justified, then, both because it is, so to speak, my subject, and because there is much subsequent reference to it by others in relation to their own preferences. It may be helpful to approach theatre in the round by way of a description of the new forms that are mentioned by the various contributors; the terminology is confusing, and the reasons for the confusion itself are interesting.

The picture-frame theatre is the common form of theatre. It has a proscenium stage, or picture-frame stage. Because it is the common form, there should be no need to give any further exposition here.

There are many new forms of theatre. In one sense most of them are in fact not new—historical precedents can usually be found; but they are certainly new in the sense that they are quite unfamiliar to most people in this country at the present time. The new forms can be distinguished from the picture-frame theatre by a single characteristic: whereas the stage of the picture-frame theatre is in one 'room' and the auditorium in another, these new forms of theatre have stage and auditorium in the same 'room'. (However, the pictorial open stage has its stage both in a separate room and in the same room as the audience.) It is worth noting that the stage of the picture-frame theatre is sometimes referred to as an enclosed stage and, for contrast, the others are therefore referred to as *open stages*. But the term *open stage* is also specifically used for the type of three-sided stage of the Shakespearian public theatre (as exemplified at Chichester). In this sense Dr Richard Southern has, for many years, used the term in his important historical writings and research work.[1] Since these new forms tend to spread the audience round the stage, and the actors are thus seen more 'three-dimensionally', the term *theatre in the round* may be given a general meaning. But it is also used, as I use

[1] See in particular, *The Open Stage*, by Richard Southern (Faber & Faber, 1953).

it, in the special sense of a theatre where the audience is spread all round a central stage.

We are used to thinking of the stage as a raised platform. But, if we are simply referring to the area on which the actors perform, there is no need for the stage to be raised. It is sometimes useful to call a stage that is not raised an *arena* or *acting area*. However, the *acting area* also means that section of an enclosed (and raised) stage where the actors perform, to distinguish it from the wing spaces and back-stage areas which are all part of the enclosed stage. Common sense must guide us here.

Another umbrella term is *arena theatre*. Mr John English has for many years directed an Arena Theatre Company which has made use of a three-sided open stage. However, in the United States the term is often used to describe a stage fully surrounded by audience; this usage is made more sensible by the series of terms: two-sided arena, three-sided arena, four-sided (or full) arena.

Each contributor to this book has used terms in his own way; but the meaning is usually clear. It is not possible to lay down the law effectively. There is no authorized usage and this cannot be expected until we have had more experience of the things themselves. I believe that the confusion of terminology is a sign of our reluctance to come to grips with new forms of theatre, and changing usage will be a natural outcome of experience. We should perhaps therefore look forward to further confusion —in hope that at least it may lead increasingly towards activity and then on to clarity.

Having sorted out, more or less, the terminology, it is now worth looking at three different examples of new forms of theatre. They make a logical sequence in terms of the extent to which the audience 'embraces' the acting area; the open end-stage, the arena stage and, finally, theatre in the round. This is also the order in which actors and audiences alike seem ready to accept them; and it follows that we have an indication here of the degree in which they break from currently accepted convention.

The Mermaid Theatre has given many people an opportunity to enjoy the open end-stage. There is a family resemblance in the temporary theatres built at Hampstead and Leicester where, in each case, the possibility of a civic theatre is on trial. The open end-stage is, fundamentally, a platform across one end of a room. The stage at the Mermaid is only a little raised—and at the Hampstead Theatre even less. The Mermaid Theatre has no stage-curtain—the other two have. But these and other differences are simply nice expressions of individuality; the form is virtually the same. In each case, a strong contact between actors and audience is possible; this is the most notable characteristic of every form of open stage and is the clear result of eschewing the proscenium wall and the separated stage behind it. However, the open end-stage does not necessarily make any new demands on the actors or producer, nor even the scene designer (though local fire regulations may impose limitations on the choice of scenic materials). It may present new opportunities, especially to the playwright, but not only must we expect to wait some time before there is a respectable body of material to identify, but also the very fact that nothing particularly new is required in presentation makes the open end-stage fairly acceptable to the theatre public and to the majority of theatre artists, and this is not likely to encourage experiment. However, the open end-stage both has its own excitement and clearly makes an essential break with the proscenium theatre.

The Festival Theatre at Chichester is described in Appendix I. It has a three-sided stage; this is an ugly term, surely 'arena stage' or 'open stage' sound better and might be preferred if only they did not also have wider connotations in common use. John English's Arena Theatre has also used this form of stage. The main differences (leaving out of consideration that the one is permanent and the other a travelling theatre) are that the former has an architectural background (which can be dismounted and replaced by scenery) and no front curtain, while the latter relies on a scenic background and makes use of a curtain. In face of widespread antipathy and apathy the Chichester theatre represents an important achievement. The respectable parentage of this form of theatre has been helpful; it has the features generally accepted as being those of Shakespeare's Globe Theatre. And, of course, the appointment of Sir Laurence Olivier as director gave assurance of success. But the first performances at this theatre were disappointingly hampered by conventional proscenium stage techniques; the experiences gained in fifteen years by John English's company were apparently ignored. Worse still, the theatre itself, in spite of many attractions, suffered from bad acoustics and poor sightlines from certain parts of the house. The limited budget on which the theatre was planned may explain inadequate accommodation back-stage (but hardly excuse it) and poor front-of-house facilities for audience; these may be improved by additional building as the theatre grows rich. But poor sightlines and acoustics in a theatre are fundamental faults. It is all the more regrettable that so many dramatic critics have drawn the conclusion that all theatres of this form must necessarily suffer from the same inadequacies and must resort to the same production tricks to overcome them. The fidgety productions of *The Chances* and *The Broken Heart* were simply beginner's mistakes. Many critics blamed the restless movement of the performers on to the form of theatre. In fact the actors were to blame, and the producer. Sir Laurence Olivier, however brilliant as an actor, has proved himself so far to be only a poor producer on this form of stage. *Uncle Vanya* was produced without concern for the open stage, and survived thanks to brilliant performances that would, by all assent, have seemed magnificent anywhere. But even in *Uncle Vanya* the absurdities were notable, particularly the use of an interior setting whose doorway between two windows led from the stage 'room' to the 'rest of the house'; it made nonsense of architecture, and of the play's storm scene, and it conflicted with the apparent intentions of producer, actors and playwright. The designer was not to blame—the vomitory entrances are available throughout the play. It is also worth remarking that most professional critics did not comment on any failure of actors or producer *vis-à-vis* the new stage; they seem to have been as ignorant as the rest. And the experience of others with this form of theatre was in no way called on during production. Muddling through remains a British panacea. It has not altogether worked. One immediate result is that the Chichester Theatre has been accepted, but the idea behind it has not, and, indeed the positive opposition to any new form of theatre may even have been strengthened. Of course it is unfair to blame the theatre for the follies of its detractors, but the faults on each side are worth noting. In the end the less publicized but more extensive work of the Arena Theatre may ensure that this form of stage is properly appreciated and developed.

The Chichester Festival Theatre and the Mermaid are the tangible products of our new interest in theatres; but in this country, as is pointed out by Professor Hunt in Appendix 2, no theatre in the round has yet been built. All the same, theatre in the round is probably talked about as much, if not more, than the other new forms of theatre.

Both the talk and the lack of action can in part be attributed to the fact that theatre in the round is an extreme form. It is fascinating to discuss, but dangerous actually to adopt in action. Whereas at the Mermaid, and even at Chichester, it is possible for the actors to perform as if they were on a picture-frame stage without the audience detecting anything odd, a performance on a central stage has to be entirely different. This is not to say that such performances at the Mermaid and Chichester are 'right'; I am quite certain they are not. The new artistic demands of the new forms of stage have simply not been adequately appreciated by most actors and producers. It should not be surprising, then, if they throw up their hands at the obvious impossibility of theatre in the round. The most that has come from talk about central staging is something *nearly* in the round; Chichester and the Mermaid are achieved on the way, as it were.

There is more to it than that. As we have seen, terminology is loose. Much talk about theatre in the round is not really about theatre in the round at all. Of course, it is quite permissible to use the term when describing an actor's performance of unusual depth and variety on any sort of stage. 'In the round' can legitimately have a very wide meaning; but it can be overworked by fashion, or by those who recognize its full implications and wish to dilute them. There has been so much talk that one might expect a theatre in the round to be built by accident if not by design. A good jibe at theatre in the round is to say, as Kenneth Tynan has done, that the only thing in its favour is that it is cheap; but one might expect several city councils to take the hint and start building at once.

Perhaps this is going too far. After all, there is nothing new about theatre in the round. Apart from the Cornish rounds and the medieval cycle of plays presented in them and the fifteenth-century evidence of *The Castle of Perseverance*,[1] there is a continuous tradition of theatre in the round for Mummers' plays and folk plays, as well as for folk-dancing, games and all sorts of sports from ancient to modern wrestling, boxing, football and so on. I guess that the amateur theatre has always used central staging; my own first sight of theatre in the round was a performance by Jack Mitchley's amateur company in Norfolk in 1948.

There has been some experiment by professional actors with theatre in the round. In 1955 the Studio Theatre Company made a temporary conversion of the Concert Room in the Central Library at Scarborough, for a summer season of plays. This theatre in the round has been erected each summer since then. The company has converted halls all over the country, for a week or two at a time, in London, Birmingham, Leicester, Newcastle-under-Lyme, Hemel Hempstead, Dartington Hall, etc. And in the autumn of 1962 the company converted an empty cinema in Stoke-on-Trent and opened it on a full-time basis. Meanwhile, the Pembroke Theatre at Croydon had opened in 1959 under the direction of Clement Scott Gilbert, and closed again after three years of exciting and flourishing existence.

The Victoria Theatre in Stoke was planned on a very limited budget, and in the event there was not even enough money to carry out the modest conversion plans completely. Paintwork and decoration were passed over, carpets were absent; audiences and actors are apparently expected to be hardy in this pristine form of theatre. The theatre itself is rectangular, with an acting area of 24 feet by 22 feet. The front row of seats is raised about 6 inches and thereafter each row is raised 1 foot 3 inches; there are five rows of seats on each of the long sides and seven at each end, accommodating 350 people. At one end of the theatre a large control-room window commands a view of the entire acting area and auditorium. There are spot bars down each of the long walls and the ceiling is pierced by two long lighting troughs and additional central squares; the ceiling spots can be reached in the roof void.

Many of the inconveniences of the place—the inadequate heating, the home-made dimmer board, the strange collection

[1] See *The Medieval Theatre in the Round* by Richard Southern (Faber).

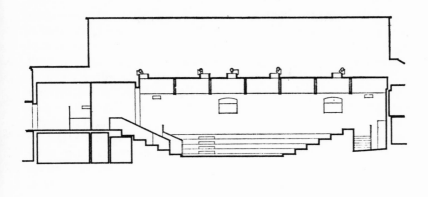

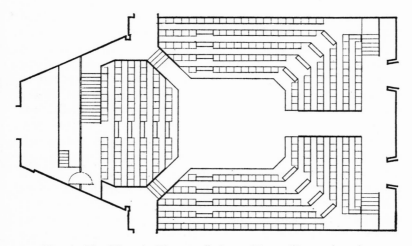

Fig. 1. The Victoria Theatre, Stoke-on-Trent. Plan and section

of sound reproducing apparatus—might be expected in any theatre opened by enthusiasts with inadequate funds. But there are certain shortcomings that belong specifically to the place as a theatre in the round. First, audience approach to seating is awkward and could be improved by an all-round gallery, such as the one devised by Stephen Garrett for the proposed theatre in the round at Newcastle-under-Lyme. This would enable people to reach (or to leave) their seats without fear of disturbing the actors, or to stand at the back of the seating and watch the play easily. Secondly, the ceiling lights work well enough, but the spot-bars on the wall are too low and have the awkward requirement of ladder access; these lights cannot be put in the roof void owing to the slope of the roof. (It may be worth remarking here that most architects, who draw plans for theatres in the round, suspend a lighting grid centrally within the plan of the acting area. They provide no access to the lights, which can therefore only be adjusted awkwardly from steps. And they provide no lighting outside the acting area; thus the actors will not be properly seen by the audience. What is a theatre for? All spotlights should be in the ceiling void which should extend far enough to give the necessary outer ring of spotlighting.) Thirdly, there are three actors' entrances, one down a slight slope and two others which must be reached by climbing three steps. The steps are awkward. Actors do not like them. In addition, actors would be greatly helped if the whole acting area were trapped so that entrances could also be made, in any part of the stage, from below. Of course, not one of these three difficulties can easily be dealt with in the existing building, which was, after all, never intended for this purpose. One hopes that anyone seriously considering building a theatre in the round will note these points, and others, learned at the Victoria Theatre. But experience shows that in theatre building we do not like to make use of experience; it is sad to think that the faults of the Victoria may well be perpetuated.

It might also be hoped that an architect designing a theatre in the round will find out from actors and technicians with the appropriate experience what their feelings and thoughts are. This is not the place to expand on the aesthetics and technicalities of central staging; it would take a book on its own. But certain obvious points, often raised, may briefly be dealt with. Many people assume that because the actor must necessarily have his back to half the audience he must keep moving so that everyone sees his face fairly frequently. (This assumption helped to mar the open-stage production of *The Chances* at Chichester.) Theatre in the round accepts it as axiomatic that everyone has a back—even actors—and that everyone knows this—even audiences. Every movement on the stage must be expressive and true. But in a theatre in the round, where there are no more than seven or eight rows, every member of the audience is close enough to observe even the subtlest of movements. So the actors' range of movement may have to be vastly extended; spatial patterns, the distances between characters, their 'line' in relation to each other and their patterns of movement, may be the means of powerful expression. So much so that some people conclude that this is a theatre for movement and for dance. Perhaps it is. Dancers are usually aware of the three-dimensional nature of space and, until trained for a Tiller chorus or for classical ballet, they resent the flatness of picture-frame staging. But this is not all the story. Theatre in the round also puts the speaking actor in the middle of his audience, and at a small enough distance for him to be heard easily (British acoustic science permitting). This is a theatre of dialectic, and Shaw's plays do very well here; it is a theatre of poetry where Shakespeare and Chekov can be presented with great lyrical sensitivity. It is not extravagant to make claims both for speech and movement. The theatre, after all, is meant to provide a feast for eye and ear. Why be surprised to find a theatre that takes this double aim seriously?

The only other point that may be broadly dealt with is the suggestion that choice of play for theatre in the round is limited. A purist may insist that a play should only be done on the sort of stage for which it is written. Dr Southern comes close to this in his warning on page 56. But how seriously does anyone believe it? As there is no theatre in the round, there are no plays written for it (writers aren't that silly); and as there are no plays written for theatre in the round, therefore there is no sense in building one. This is a good argument for preserving the *status quo*. Actually it isn't quite true, of course, since many plays have already been written for the theatre in the round run by the Studio Theatre Company. But apart from theatre in the round, are we to have no Shakespeare on picture-frame stages? Have the Old Vic and Stratford-on-Avon been guilty for so many years of sacrilege? After no end of discussion there is room for many points of view. Dr Guthrie is surely right to present a classical and modern repertoire at his new pictorial open stage in Minneapolis; the main consideration is simply this—a good play is always worth doing on any form of stage. Maybe some plays will go better on one form of stage than on another, but more likely this will remain a matter of opinion. It is good that it should be so. Let us, in the theatre, exercise our individual tastes; we should have the opportunity to choose and to enjoy all sorts of plays in all sorts of theatres. Only a feeble public needs to be spoon-fed by critical nannies and ordered a restricted diet by careful pedants.

To return to architecture, a final comment should be made about the cheapness of theatre in the round. I expect it is quite true that open stages can, seat for seat, be built cheaper than picture-frame stages. But money can be wasted by the shilling as well as by the pound, and efficiency has a price. It is possible to spend millions of pounds on any building and do it badly; it is possible to have a small budget and still waste it on inefficiency. A good architect, it is hoped, will achieve good results on either scale, but there is a limit below which even a theatre in the round cannot be built.

IV

The three forms discussed so far by no means exhaust the possibilities, which are, of course, limitless. But these three, together with the picture-frame stage, are of immediate concern in that they find their separate ways on to the architect's drawing-board. Together they offer a challenge to the architect who tries to accommodate them all in the same building. The idea of a theatre complex, where several different forms of stage are grouped in relation to common back-stage accommodation and front-of-house facilities, can scarcely be explored where the demand for theatre is limited. An alternative is to have an adaptable theatre where a single volume can house each form of stage and the apparatus necessary to bring the change from one form to another.[1] Where only two forms are contemplated, as at Nottingham, not much machinery may be required, and when the theatre is small, as with the LAMDA studio, very little apparatus need be used. The LAMDA theatre can provide a picture-frame stage, open stage or theatre in the round by means of mobile seating blocks and curtains. The changeover can be effected in a short time, say ten minutes. This is ideal for a dramatic training school. The Questors Theatre achieves adaptability with portable rostrum units and movable panels; this is an amateur theatre where there is a reliable labour force. But the Questors is still a small theatre. The Nottingham Theatre is on an altogether larger scale, and the adaptability is more limited. To build a large, fully adaptable theatre would probably cost more, in machinery, than the sum necessary to build the separate components. And its attractions are therefore limited. However, the small adaptable theatre has obvious advantages and it is likely to appeal to training schools, universities, amateur groups and organizations where many different people are concerned with the presentation of many different plays.

If there are many different forms of theatre how is one to choose between them? The question arises immediately a new building is contemplated. First of all it depends who *one* is. A theatre nowadays is unlikely to be built by one person and, if it is, he will probably have strong ideas of his own ; he will not read a book for guidance. More likely a theatre will be built by a committee, a council perhaps, or a trust. Many interests may have to be considered, from the various preferences of committee members to the desires of the people who will work in the theatre. Now it is likely that most members of a civic committee will know little about theatre. It is also likely that the people who will eventually work in the theatre have not yet been appointed; if an old theatre already exists and is being replaced, the people who work in it may either go elsewhere for their next job, or, more often, those who will stay to work in the new theatre may have little experience or understanding of anything other than the old theatre itself. A committee should, of course, take into account the views of these people, and they may need to seek no further. But there are other important

[1] See 'Adaptable Theatres' edited by Stephen Joseph, *ABTT*, 1962.
A A A—C

issues which everyone concerned must consider. They cannot be dealt with briefly, but, roughly speaking, four groups of questions indicate the first decisions to be made. Firstly, there are questions relating to usage, such as: What is the purpose of the theatre in terms of actors? Will it have a permanent company, touring companies, plays or ballet, opera and orchestral concerts? Next, there are questions relating to the audience and to expected ticket sales. How big should it be to fulfil its purpose? To balance its budget (taking subsidies into consideration)? To cater for the potential audience? Financial questions are likely to be more complex, but may take the form: How much money can be spent on the building? And subsequently on maintaining it and running it? Lastly, and of varying importance, the starting point of the building itself: What is the nature of the site? Or is there a suitable site available? Many of these questions depend on each other and the answers may not be easy to reach. There are bodies such as the Arts Council, the Theatres Advisory Council, and the Association of British Theatre Technicians, each of which may offer helpful advice. A professional theatre consultant can be called in to help the client in choosing his theatre and to advise the architect in detailing it. An architect must be expected to have difficulty in designing a theatre well unless he is told precisely what it is for. He should not be relied on to design a theatre better than his brief; he may do so, but he will be more likely to design well if the brief is good. It is in the preparation of the brief for the architect that the success or failure of the building is likely to lie, and in many ways committee organization is well-suited to the purpose, provided advice is sought from different sources and listened to with keenness.

As far as new forms of theatre are concerned, obviously there is a strong likelihood that they will not be seriously considered. The reasons have already been noted. However, the idea of a new form may arise in a special way. The committee may have the wisdom to appoint the director of the new theatre before the brief is prepared. (Where the director is appointed subsequently he may wish to alter the plans of the new building.) The best candidate for the job might be in favour of a new theatre form. The committee may back his judgement, and their task would now be straightforward. The temptation to compromise would always be there, and compromise could be fairly relied on to lead to a result unsatisfactory to all parties, though it might by chance produce an interesting theatre that no one had thought of. It would be an unwise gamble to expect this, of course. The safer plan is to back one man's judgement, especially if he is to use the theatre.

But is it advisable to build a highly idiosyncratic theatre? Would it be wise to appoint a director with extremist views? It is true that the director may not hold the appointment for long and that another director might require something different. The policy of production may be determined by the theatre form; should this be left more open, or brought more in line with most other theatres? In the end there is no doubt that it depends on the people concerned; but there is absolutely nothing wrong with a highly idiosyncratic theatre provided that its implications are understood. Even a theatre must have a limited life, and to build a theatre for eternity is impossible anyhow. Fashions in drama change; so should theatre buildings. Finally, since the likelihood of building a new form of theatre is so remote the important thing to do here is to put forward the less heard argument. An outstandingly original and well-built theatre will give distinction to any city in England. It will shine like a good deed.

Both client and architect may tend to approach the idea of building a theatre with a vision of permanence. But the drama is an ephemeral art. It is important to build with conviction for today's drama. Yesterday's drama is of less importance and anyhow we always have yesterday's theatres with us. No one can build for tomorrow's drama with assurance; though obviously tomorrow's drama will arrive, if it arrives at all, in today's theatres. Efficiency is more important than permanence. And if we are to build today's theatres efficiently, more needs to be known about the choice available to us.

V

There is always a danger in discussing theatre seriously that we shall seem more than a little absurd, quite apart from any personal shortcomings. For surely the main function of drama is to provide mere entertainment? And, at any rate in these days, it apparently entertains only a small number of people. Paradoxically there are plenty of applicants for places at the dramatic training schools but too few people are available to fill the seats in the auditoriums. The administration and business of theatre is usually so badly organized that few people with talent and intelligence are ready to devote their time to it; only a small proportion of workers in the theatre are well paid (and some of these are grossly overpaid), and most people who depend on the theatre for a living are neither particularly talented nor intelligent, and they are usually underpaid and overworked. So why not let the theatre alone to dwindle away? The answer is that it simply won't dwindle away. Its present sorry plight is due to our bad treatment, not to the theatre itself. We have pushed it into hard times and mean surroundings which have obscured its value, or we have tried to turn it into a commercial commodity. That it survives at all is an indication of hardiness. If we have any sense we shall try to rediscover its value. In chapters 5 and 6 of this book two such attempts are made; firstly, to state the significance of drama as a spiritual force, and secondly, to show that, on this level, it will soon be a necessity to us when we are forced to come to grips with the new problem of leisure.

As our society increases its control over materials we all, more or less, benefit from higher standards of living; our hours of leisure have increased and are still increasing. But the steadfast materialism of this phase in our social development will not be sufficient to cope with our new leisure. Man cannot, as it were, live by washing-machines alone. We may try to take the easy way out by ensuring that most of our human nature is stunted, by turning the imaginative human being into a mindless animal. Indeed, much of our educational system has been geared for this purpose; in the past the arts have been available to the aristocratic few or to the privileged middle-classes, while working people, in our stratified society, have been prepared by their education for conditions of work which will deprive them of pleasure in the arts. The arts have responded accordingly. But surely we do not want to deny ourselves the exercise of our natural faculties? It is not a matter, then, of 'educating' people so that they can join the privileged ranks of, for instance, theatre-goers. The theatre can speak, if we allow it, to all people; we have only to take it out of its fetters. We must let the theatre expand, we must explore it, we must allow it to grow. There is, after all, nothing 'mere' about entertainment; it is a phenomenon that shows mankind enjoying his humanity. Drama has long been recognized by poets and philosophers as the essence of civilization. This is why it is worth taking seriously. Actors and architects should keep this in mind.

2

Theatre at Minneapolis

TYRONE GUTHRIE

I AM going to start with a few general remarks about theatre architecture, and then I am going to tell you specifically something about the theatre that is now being built in Minneapolis, more or less (so far as the stage is concerned) to the specification of Miss Moiseiwitsch and myself. But first a few general remarks. One can't, of course, at this juncture, expect architects, when they're asked to build a theatre, to be on very familiar territory. They are all building coke ovens and atomic reactor stations, houses for rich widows and council flats for workers, and things like that, a mile a minute. And on those kind of things naturally one expects them to have a high degree of expertise. But should an architect be lucky enough to be asked to design a theatre, naturally he's on less familiar territory. And if it's a fairly monied employer, what he does is to say, 'Well, please may I have a substantial cheque to send me abroad to look at theatres?' If I were the employer I would immediately say, 'You can look at pictures of theatres, and the money that you would spend travelling around from Mannheim to Oslo, and from Oslo to the Mediterranean, and from the Mediterranean to Ankara, and then to the mid-west of America, is going into the building which you will provide the plans for. So far as all that is concerned, you just write to the various people who have built theatres in the last decade, and get them to send you their plans (which they will be proud to do), and look at the photographs which can be found in any well-equipped Public Library under various very peculiar headings.' What do you learn from going to look at these places? An architect should be able to read a plan. *I* can't but *he's* trained to. And even I can look at pictures and can tell at a glance, for instance, that the Frank Lloyd Wright theatre at Dallas is just no good. It's very handsome, it's madly

30

expensive, but it makes what I think is the cardinal mistake—
of thinking that there is a merit in having the largest possible
cubic space with the smallest possible number of human beings
in it. It is axiomatic in my philosophy of the theatre that the
audience has got to be packed into the place. The rapport
between the stage and the audience is tremendously conditioned
by the amount of cubic space that is empty. The Royal Opera
House at Covent Garden, which I think is a beast of a building,
is considered very distinguished. So I am sure it is on gala nights
when the Queen is there in jewels like stop-and-go lights and
there are Field Marshals a mile a minute in their feathers. On
nights like that it is great. But when you or I are there with
mackintoshes on, and a bag of brussels sprouts on the floor
between us, you're conscious that this is a great Sahara of red
velvet. The amount of empty air is tremendous; it is fighting
the performance all the time.

What I would demand of an architect, were it mine to be
choosing somebody, would be some philosophy of the theatre
that we shared, some idea of what was the purpose of performance and what were the sort of ideas to which performance
should aspire. Then set him to work to create a building in
which those things could be realized. But too often architects
pay tremendous attention to the wishes of their patron, who is
probably somebody like the Chancellor of a University, or the
head of a County Council, or the Lord Mayor of a big city, or
somebody who is just there because he is the Chairman of the
relevant Committee (not because he really is expert or even
vitally interested), and he will suggest that there should be a
suitable retiring room with the right facilities, and that the
foyer should be handsomely decorated—and irrelevances like
that. In my experience the architects who are set to do this for
their new chore, make the most minimal consultation with the
kind of people they ought to consult first, last and all the way
along the line—the people who have got to work in the building,
notably the stage managers. Some of the theatres that have
been put up, great and small, in this country since the war,
have made elementary mistakes such as not having a wide
enough door between the scene-painting place and the stage
(so that everything has to be up-ended, 'To you', 'To me', 'To
you', and handled fifteen times, before it makes the journey,

which it was destined from the beginning to make, from the paintshop to the stage; and back again to the paintshop). Architects forget the actors completely. I am now thinking of what is in my opinion the very, very badly designed building in Coventry, the Belgrade Theatre; it has the handsomest foyer in the land, the chandeliers are great, but that isn't what anybody goes to the theatre to see. It was designed to be a repertory theatre. Well now, surely the people who must be considered first in the repertory theatre are members of the public. But giving them a lovely chandelier isn't quite the point. They could get that at the local hotel. What they want to have is somewhere where the plays can be seen to the best advantage. After the public, and I am not sure that in practical ways they are not the first people to be considered, are the lower classes who are going to work there, the slaves of the lamp! But, for instance, the dressing-rooms are very ill equipped with fresh air and daylight. Indeed, engineers can say till they are blue in the face that the stuff that squirts out of an air conditioning vent or duct may be the purest ozone, but psychologically it is not. It may be doing one's lungs a great amount of good, but it is desperately depressing to the spirit. And if you are in the theatre, as a repertory actor is, from half-past nine in the morning till half-past eleven at night it is essential that during your rests and your waits you should be refreshed. If you are a small part player you will probably have to come on and say 'My Lord, the carriage awaits', and then twenty-eight pages later you come on and say, 'Long reign the Queen of Barataria.' And during these twenty-eight pages it is essential that you should get out and read your paper in a sunny room, or at least in a daylit room. These are the kind of things that architects should ask about. But they very rarely do. The architect should get in touch with a good, experienced old professional and say to him, 'Will you please tell me how to design the prompt corner; where the switches ought to be? Will you explain to me what goes on in the prompt corner? Will you allow me to come and watch you in the prompt corner when a performance is going on?' But those kinds of practical detail, in so far as my experience is concerned, are almost completely neglected.

In Canada, since the war, in the big mid-western cities, Calgary, Winnipeg and Alberta (and I think Vancouver too) they have put up giant Concert Halls. But they are all-purpose halls, which are, *a priori*, no-purpose halls. They hold 3,500 people, which means that the human being is completely lost. The stages are something like sixty feet wide, which is twice the width of Her Majesty's Theatre in London. An actor on that stage looks like a peanut. You can sit in the front row and the corner people in the same row are half an acre away in one direction and half an acre in the other direction. It is no sort of view. They think that 3,500 people are going to come to the performances (and they very often do, because if they don't go there they don't go anywhere), and they expect a lot of money to be made; so, a lot of money has been spent on *de-luxe* equipment. The managers, who in every case are municipal authorities, pride themselves on the star dressing-rooms, which are equipped with tables for massage, and electric appliances of every possible kind; a telephone in the lavatory (private of course), as well as a telephone in the dressing-room, and a telephone in the enormous room where the Star is supposed to receive the bouquets and the press. But the lower classes, again, just work in concentration camps, three floors below ground, heaped like sardines into a totally unequipped cellar. All these things are out of date. It suggests the romantic idea of some architect who is fascinated by the Star side of the theatre, who has probably read film-star magazines in his teen-age years, and who has not taken sufficiently into account the professional routine of the theatre.

Well, with those unkind words to the architectural profession, I shall now proceed to describe to you the theatre which is now being built in Minneapolis, and why it is being built as it is.

The brief to my partners and myself, passed on by us to the architect, was that this should be a theatre where a classical rep can be done. Minneapolis is a big place. Minneapolis and St Paul are really one city, but, you know, it's like Edinburgh and Glasgow, or Dublin and Belfast—just because they are so close there is intense rivalry. I suppose one could almost say Manchester and Liverpool, but it is as though Manchester and Liverpool, instead of being forty-five miles apart, were actually locked together. Where St Paul merges into Minneapolis is only clear if you have the map open in front of you. Logically you would think that the Mississippi River, which flows through the middle on its serpentine course, would divide the two, that one city would be on one bank and the other on the other. But it is not as simple as that because the river is very wriggly and the bits in between are sometimes one city and sometimes the other. Incidentally, I think the great charm of this place, and why it came historically into being, is that it was the last place which big boats could get up to before the river became unnavigably shallow. It is 4,000 miles from the sea. It is as though the Irwell were to be infinitely prolonged and were to come out to the sea at Baghdad. The sea is that far away! Through the city, through great gorges with parks on either side, the river is as wide as the Thames at Waterloo Bridge, and five times as turbulent. It is quite a thrilling location. But that is all by the way.

This is a city that has, as American cities go, a reputation for culture. It has a symphony orchestra of world renown that has been going for a great many years. It used to have, in the days of stock companies, a famous stock company, one of the best in the United States, long gone. It is badly placed for theatrical touring, because it is a very long haul from there to the next place. It is the last big city before you get to the coast, and the coast is two days and a night away by train and a good many hours by plane. The situation is isolated from Minneapolis westward. And from Minneapolis eastward it is an overnight journey to Chicago, and forty-seven hours by train from New York, five or six by Jet. It is almost as far on again from New York as New York is from London. For many years they have had a dwindling, and a never very strong supply of touring attractions. The touring theatre in the United States is largely packing up. Nothing tours, nothing can afford to tour, that is not a cast-iron box office proposition; *My Fair Lady, West Side Story*, that kind of thing; hardly any straight plays can afford to tour. The journeys are too great. And anyway plays seldom do good business because the touring theatres are so enormous. We have all been spoilt by movies; perhaps our eyes have been opened by the movies and television. We expect to see the actors, we expect to hear them, so spoilt are we. And if you are sitting at the back of a theatre that holds 3,000 people you don't see the actors at all, and you only hear them if they are relayed by a loudspeaker. It is a disappointing and dreary experience which people simply do not support. So they have seen nothing, theatrically, for many years except very sporadic tours, almost entirely of musical comedies from the East. But you can't push a pin between the amateur dramatic societies, whose standard is very variable. There is an excellent Jewish company that does good plays and does them well. Then there are various church societies that do rubbish disgracefully; and there is an Operatic Society. There is a small outcrop of summer stock in the suburbs in what are meant to be picturesque surroundings, which are not good; they do the Broadway successes of yester-year, with young aspiring companies, mostly, I would say, with a standard not the equal of our best reps, perhaps a little better than our worst reps. But not an exciting standard. They were eager enough, so starved for theatre were they, that it has been possible to raise by local subscription entirely two and a quarter million dollars to build the new theatre, which is a remarkably big sum when dug out of private pockets, in a city not by any means as big as Manchester. The total population is half a million and there are no outskirts. There is nothing corresponding to the big cities within hailing distance of Manchester. There are small towns sixty, seventy, eighty miles away, but otherwise, nothing for hundreds of miles.

It seemed to us that the right policy to pursue was not to condescend. One must not assume because they haven't had a theatre that they are not capable of appreciating the best. But they haven't seen anything; therefore, it seemed (as I am to be the artistic director, I may as well say it seemed to me, since mine was the dominant voice on the Council) that the right thing to do was to try and offer a programme which made no concessions in regard to quality. They had better see what posterity had considered the best, in other words a classical programme, but 'classical' interpreted widely. America hasn't been going long enough to develop any classics in drama. Plays written in America, until about 1920, were completely derivative from the European Theatre and mostly treated of European subjects. From O'Neill onwards there have developed a number of authors who, I think, could be regarded fairly enough as aspirants, likely contenders, for the classical status; and in any given season we intend to do one American play which cannot be called a classic but which any reasonable person would say was a possible contender for classical status. For the rest, plays of unquestionable status, but not all English. Without your knowing about the rep I can't explain to you the kind of conditions which governed the plans for the building. The first season we are going to open with *Hamlet*; next a translation of *L'Avare* by Molière, then *The Three Sisters* of Chekov and last, as our American play, *The Death of a Salesman*.

Now the first question that confronted us, in connection with the design of the theatre, was how big was it to be? And it seemed to us that it ought to hold not less than a thousand people, not simply and solely for financial reasons, but because if you have a too small theatre you tend to generate a small response. If your potential audience is small naturally you have to scale down your theatre, because you can't expect to fill it. If you put into a town of 10,000 a theatre holding 1,000 that would be crazy. But in a great city it seemed to us that we would be doing poorly, our status would be pretty low, if, including the visitors who will certainly be attracted (this is a whole region, thousands of square miles, which is completely starved of theatres, in a way which in the British Isles it is hardly possible to conceive of, and we are obviously going to get a considerable number of visitors), it seemed pessimistic to assume that we couldn't fill a proportion of a thousand seats. And for big plays, such as we are doing, you need a pretty powerful heavyweight response which is largely a matter of numbers. Then came the financial considerations. The public has raised the money to build the theatre, and we feel it is desirable (though not absolutely essential) that we should make the operation pay its way. But I do not want to put too much stress on that, because it seems to be as foolish in the modern era to expect a serious theatre to pay as it would be to expect an art gallery to pay, or a hospital to pay, or a church to pay. The quality of the thing simply must not be judged on the quantitative response of the public. What is being dealt with is too serious for that. If the thing *never* attracts then it's not wanted by the public. It had better fade away. But if what is being done is any good, from time to time certain of its attractions will be madly popular and the quantitative response will be very large. But one will never in the modern world draw huge houses (except with very exceptional circumstances like a remarkable star performance) to the *Spook Sonata* of Strindberg. It is just not for a large public. Yet it is the kind of thing that any serious repertory theatre ought to include in its programme. Here one is not aiming primarily at a large public, but at a serious minority public and to set standards. However, be that as it may, we settled for about a thousand people.

It is my impression that a thousand people cannot be got near enough to the actors for really intimate effects to be achieved unless they are put to some extent around the stage. The ordinary theatre as we know it is a box. The stage area occupies about half the space. On it there is a barrier of scenery which leaves wing space, and back-stage space. Between the two halves of the box there is a barrier of fire, called the footlights, then a barrier of space called the orchestra. (This is not really designed as a theatre so much as an opera house.) In this other half is where the public sits, facing one way, and generally in several tiers, with the circles arranged more or less facing the stage. I guess I need not say much about how this came into being. It spread all over Europe, about the middle of the seventeenth century, for the very good reason that at that time the whole of Europe, and shortly afterwards the British Isles, were just crazy about the Italian opera, the musical drama, drama sung with orchestral accompaniment. And for sung drama with orchestral accompaniment this is a very sensible and logical layout. The orchestra sits down in the pit, the conductor sits facing the same way as the audience where he can command the stage, and hold the performance together; the actors face the other way, so that they can be best heard, and the expressions on their lovely faces can be best seen. And even more important, they can see the conductor, and 'get the beat'. That is very, very sensible for opera. And it is sensible for the sort of plays that develop in that particular kind of theatre. It has one big disadvantage. It is a very uneconomic use of cubic space. The auditorium is planned with rows that go one way and aisles that go the other way. The circles come round, but only part of the way, because, if you bring them round too far, the lines of sight from a corner seat would leave a very large amount of the stage out of sight. One of the best intimate proscenium theatres is the Lyceum, Edinburgh. The line of sight from the circle there is such that somebody on the side (and I have often sat in such a seat) is only able to see a small portion of the stage. This is nothing unusual. In the Metropolitan Opera House, New York, six hundred seats can't see the stage, at all. The Old Vic, which probably a good many of you have been in, holds just under a thousand, and nobody could say that it was a very intimate playhouse. It is reasonably intimate. But that's all it holds.

Now if you design a theatre so that the audience comes much further round the stage, immediately the capacity is tremendously increased. Let me give you tangible proof of this. The theatre in Stratford, Ontario, with its open stage, seats 2,225 people in no more than thirteen rows. The theatre is planned on a circle of which just under half is back-stage area. The stage sticks out into the auditorium rather like a peninsula; and the aisles of the theatre are designed to come in like the radii of a circle. The seats go round in semicircles. Now the back rows will clearly hold more than three times as many seats as if they were arranged laterally—as they would be in the proscenium theatre. This is a theatre which holds 2,225 people and the furthest row from the stage is row M, i.e. thirteen rows back, which is less than half-way back compared with the Opera House in, say, Manchester. And even at row M it is a little too deep. Intimacy is not sufficient. I think eleven or even ten rows would be right. But you can by this means, and, I think, by this means alone, combine intimacy with large capacity.

So our problem at Minneapolis was can we do a classical rep in those circumstances? What of the big classics are suited to the open stage, what are unsuited? Now it is my contention that anything is suited that was written for some such a stage. And for some such a stage, not precisely similar but much more similar than the opera house set-up, is everything that was written for the theatre from the Greeks until the suppression of the theatre in this country by the puritans; that is to say Shakespeare, and everything that preceded Shakespeare, and Shakespeare's immediate successors. After that plays tended to be written for the proscenium. The next point is, which of the proscenium written plays can be pulled out into the open without doing them violence? My contention is that a great many can, and a great many more than conservative people suppose. Personally, I haven't experimented very much with this. My

PLATE IV

Stratford Shakespearean
Festival Theatre,
Ontario: interior

(*Left to right*):
Brian Jackson, associate
    designer
Tanya Moiseiwitsch,
    designer
Michael Langham,
    artistic director

Photograph by Peter Smith

PLATE V
Stratford Shakespearean
Festival Theatre,
Ontario:
a scene from
Cyrano de Bergerac,
directed by
Michael Langham

experience of this kind of stage has been confined to Stratford, Ontario, where I have done *Oedipus Rex* of Sophocles and several Shakespeare plays. And I have seen a number of Shakespeare plays, and I have seen *Cyrano de Bergerac*; I would have thought *Cyrano de Bergerac* was one of the very last plays which you could pull out on to a stage of this kind, that it demanded glamour, and illusion; because, let's face it, it is just a musical comedy without music. But it was marvellously directed. The performance was a tremendous popular success. I thought the play was rubbish before I saw it; I thought the play was rubbish while it was going on; and I thought the play rubbish after thinking it over. But that doesn't mean that a good time wasn't had by all. The snuffles, the handkerchiefs out, the carries-on in the last act! The pathos, which you wouldn't have thought was very easy to achieve when the actor was dying three feet from the nearest people! A brilliant star performance by Christopher Plummer! But I would have thought it was one of the very last kinds of plays which you could do on the open stage. Laurence Olivier demonstrated to most people's satisfaction at Chichester last summer that *Uncle Vanya* could come out and be done that way. To me it was no surprise; it didn't seem odd. I always thought Chekov could be done on the open stage. I am quite convinced that all the later plays of Ibsen can, and I suspect that such realistic social documents as *The Wild Duck* and *The Doll's House* can, because all you are doing is depriving them of surrounding walls; the furniture can be arranged in a way more realistically than it can behind a proscenium. And I feel that the intimate contact of the artist with the audience is an advantage not a disadvantage. I have seen, off Broadway, a fairly inadequate production of *Rosmersholm* done completely in the round. I must say I didn't think the production was very good (but I didn't think it would have been very good in any circumstances) and being in the round didn't seem to me to do the play any harm. You certainly lost something of the feeling of oppression, the claustrophobia which a box set could give; but there were other compensating advantages, and I thought that if the acting had been a little better the claustrophobia could have been presented there rather than in paint and canvas. However, be that as it may, my own view is that there are certain kinds of play which it would be madness to play on an open stage. Broadly speaking, the plays that I think would be no good in such circumstances are all the artificial comedies, from Restoration comedy down to the end of the eighteenth century. A great deal in them depends upon the artists playing one another off against the audience—being able to say something to the collaborator on the stage and turn to the audience and say 'Little does he know!' which doesn't, I think, work very happily in the round or the near round. Maybe I'm wrong, but to me the charm of Restoration comedy is its removal from life, that it is these periwigged, big-flounced, extremely artificial creations standing up in artificial light, carrying on in no realistic way at all, but in a highly stylistic—almost operatic— presentation of life. But nearly all the great Victorians could come out in the open. And, for our purpose in America, it seemed to us that for ten years at least we must certainly keep English Restoration comedy out of the rep because what does it mean to the Middle West? You must know something about London, and American actors are just not equipped to act it at the moment. They don't speak in the right style. They have no sympathy with it. They haven't the sort of accomplishment that it demands. They have other virtues, plenty of them, but the particular sort of skill which Edith Evans so wonderfully exemplifies in our theatre just is not at their command. No doubt there are some actors who can do it, but they are very few and far between and we didn't think we could come upon them. And we didn't think there was any great demand for such service for some time to come. And we did not think there was going to be any great loss if we have to omit them for the present. Can we do Sheridan, let us say, and even Goldsmith? They are extremely English. They haven't much to say to the Middle West. Just because I come from Britain it is extremely important that I don't seem to be shoving British products down their throats. The American theatre is always being grand-mothered by us. We come over and say 'Old darlings, you really don't know anything about it! We have been at it for five centuries. Let me show you!' And it doesn't do. These are grown-up people who are developing their own theatre. If you are going to work in the Middle West this must be, as quickly as it can become so, an expression of the Middle West. So, to cut a long story short, we decided that the things that simply couldn't be done on the open stage were probably not things, in short term, we would want to do anyway; and, in long term, the theatre could probably get along without them in the foreseeable future.

It was considered long and earnestly whether you could combine the two forms of theatre. We stewed over the plans of the big American National Theatre which is going to be built at the Lincoln Centre. This does attempt to combine the two. You press an electronic this and you pull a something else that, and lo and behold! a whole lot of seats shuffle out of sight and disappear into thin air. An apron stage thrusts itself forward. And there you are in another kind of form. On paper it is extremely ingenious. I could be very wrong, the last thing I want to be is dogmatic about this, but my belief is that it is neither as good as it could be as a proscenium theatre, nor as good as it could be as an open stage; that, in order to get the flexibility of changing between the two, you have to spend a great deal of money on buttons and machinery and so on, and, when it has all occurred, it is still a compromise, an exceedingly clever compromise but unmistakably a compromise; it isn't quite a proscenium theatre when it is being a proscenium and it isn't a fully effective open stage when it is being open. One could be very wrong. I am not good at reading plans, but I have seen it in plan, I have seen it in elevation, I have heard it enthusiastically described by its only begetters, and I am quite unconvinced. We thought, for better or for worse, we would plunge without compromise for one or the other, and we have plunged for the open stage because, as I say, the things that one thought couldn't be done there don't seem very relevant to the repertoire, and the things that we are going to do nearly all seem to want the open stage. Above all you get this extremely close relationship, geographically close, between the audience and the actors.

Now it is perfectly true that if you are working on an open stage a certain amount of masking has to take place, and a certain amount of turning has to take place. The masking can be avoided to a very considerable extent. When the stage juts forward and the audience is all around it, masking can be avoided if there are steps all the way round, and if the flat area is comparatively reduced. Now this would not work for a room.

If a room has to be presented, it cannot be all up and down steps, but for Shakespeare it is fine. Henry V stands on the top level and the troops are all around him, lower down, so that Henry can be seen addressing them. The throne is set anywhere near the centre and the courtiers are on a lower level. It is a simple solution, but it really works. It is perfectly true that wherever you stand on such a stage, your back is going to be to somebody in the audience. That can be got round by turning.

I didn't go to Chichester but everybody tells me that they thought the productions there were terribly restless. My productions at Stratford, Ontario, may have been restless, but I can say that Michael Langham's are not. Under his direction actors have learnt how to manage. When we were first considering the open stage, I set myself the little exercise of speaking something which, it seemed to me, ought to be spoken still and not moving, like 'To be or not to be . . .' and seeing if, in front of a glass, I could get this spread around an arc of 180 degrees without seeming to be restless. I haven't any great talent as an actor, but I thought to my own satisfaction I was able to do it without being restless. The trick of it seemed to be to begin in an easy way on one side, and then to turn first one's eyes and then one's head and then very slowly one's shoulders and then, hardly moving the feet at all, just by turning the shoulders, one was able to get round to the other side and let them see what one's eyes were expressing. In fact I think that is true. I don't believe that people need keep spinning about on their feet in order to direct the thing round a segment of 180 degrees. It is a slightly different technique from that of working in a proscenium theatre, but I think it imposes less artificiality on the actor.

Let us take the instance of a Shakespeare scene. You all know the kind of way that Shakespeare has to be done on the proscenium stage. King Henry comes on accompanied by my Lords of Norfolk, Suffolk, Arundel, Abergavenny and all points west, six or seven of them, and they have to come on from one side. The most important person gets in the centre, and up-stage, and the others (there is no way out of this) have to make a kind of arrow shape. It couldn't be more artificial. That is how the scene is going to be played on a proscenium stage. But if five or six people gather round a focal point in reality they are going to gather round in a circle. I don't mean literally a circle, but the general effect is of gathering all round a focal point. And that is precisely what you cannot do on a proscenium stage because of the lines of sight and the masking; but you can do it on an open stage. They can come round on the steps below and they can even get up behind him on top. Whatever the point of interest, be it a throne or a bed or a new-born baby, that is how in fact one arranges oneself. You gather in a fire-lit room around the fire, and there is no getting away from it that in the proscenium theatre the pretence of putting the fireplace in the footlights is a very unsatisfactory one. Nobody believes that if a semicircle of actors form up to face the audience they are sitting around the fireside. They just look as though at any moment they are going to burst into the auditorium. Put the fire to one side or the other and, if they face the fire, they are facing away from the audience and masking one another. My belief is that on the open stage, rooms can be set up. You can set up your furniture as though it were a real room with no fourth wall. There are no walls. And you arrange your furniture, with sofas, chairs, and all the appurtenances, so that the people do roughly get into a circle, facing one another. And it is perfectly clear that a member of the audience sitting in one particular place can only see the back of that particular actress's head, and only such portion of her back as appears over the back of the sofa. The answer to that is that no one must get stuck in the sofa for too long. But it is surprising how much can be expressed with the back of a head.

I would like to tell you very briefly how the stage in Minneapolis will be arranged, and what the back of the stage will be. The same team is designing the stage as designed Stratford, Ontario—myself and Miss Moiseiwitsch—and we feel that we have learnt lessons from Stratford, Ontario; we may have learnt the wrong lessons (that remains to be seen) but we feel certain things have been found out, and we hope to correct certain mistakes. Also, Ontario was designed with the limited objective of being a Shakespeare Festival Theatre. Occasionally and, as the years go on, more and more they will widen their repertoire. It will still be based on Shakespeare and the stage has to be suitable for Shakespeare. The Stratford stage comes out into the house, with four steps leading up to it all the way round. At the back there is a triangular-shaped balcony, with pillars. There are two tunnel entrances from below up a slope. Four rows back, you go under the auditorium down a steep slope and into a tunnel. These are vitally important entrances. You can enter underneath the balcony by coming either side of each pillar, or you can get on to the top of the balcony, or there are side doors. It has been slightly modified this year, but in principle it is much the same. The balcony is permanent, and this, I think, is almost necessary for Shakespeare.

In Minneapolis, we thought that the balcony could not be permanent. It would only be a nuisance. What is the alternative? Well, I must now try to describe the back wall of the stage. It will be roughly rectangular. The theory is that it should not be a scene, that that space must not be representational. It must not be like the back scene of a representational stage. The representing must happen on the stage in front, where the actors are. It is to be a corrugated wall, and in it are doors, and windows. These will be cabinet-made so that they are flush when closed. They can all be opened as either doors or windows, and you can set a staircase to form a balcony. Then the whole wall divides down the middle and will open like garage doors. It will not reveal another picture behind— lo and behold! we are in another part of the forest! It will simply part in order to belch out a truck, so that you can change the scenery, not quite instantaneously, but in a matter of seconds. Between the acts of, let us say, a Chekov play, a truck can come out on lines from between those doors; it is set up with sofas, tables, standard lamps, just as a tea-tray is set up with a teapot, milk jug, and cups and saucers. Then it can be retracted at the end of the act. Debate ranged as to whether this should be a very costly electronic mechanism; you pressed a button and it came out by unseen hands. And we thought that was a very silly way to spend some thousands of dollars. Why was it better for the hands to be unseen? Nobody would suppose it was anything but a truck on which chairs and tables were set. What was wrong with a couple of men in white coats just shoving it out, at infinitely less expense? That, in fact, is what is going to happen.

There is no pretence that this is magic. You see, the whole

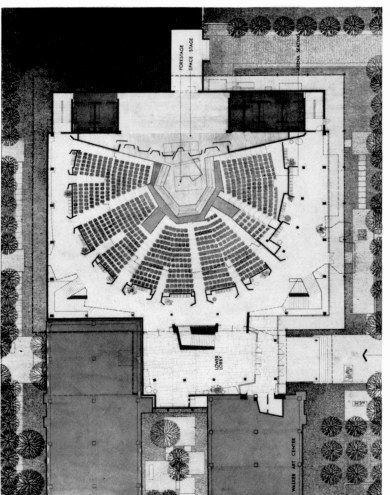

FORESTAGE

SPACE STAGE

ARENA SEATING

LOWER
LOBBY

WALKER ART CENTER

Architects: Ralph Rapson, Minneapolis

PLATE VI
Plan of the
Tyrone
Guthrie
Theatre,
Minneapolis

PLATE VII
Interior of the
Tyrone
Guthrie
Theatre:
a scene from
*The Three
Sisters*
by the
Minnesota
Theatre
Company

idea of the thing is not to create illusion—I don't believe that is what the theatre is about. I don't believe people go to the theatre to be presented with a palpable fiction and think it's really happening. Very unsophisticated people no doubt do; and young children do. But from a very early age young children begin to rumble that Peter Pan is an elderly lady, and that she is flying on a wire. And the grown-up audience, I don't believe for a moment, is pursuaded that this palpable fiction is reality, any more than when one reads a novel one really thinks that the events in it are happening. If it is a good enough novel you are completely carried away, you are lost in a world of imagination. Take the other analogy, with painting. When you go to the Louvre and look at the *Mona Lisa*, you don't think that she is a real lady looking at you. You know perfectly well that it is a painting of a lady. There is no illusion. You look at it and you are interested or not according to the degree in which you are fascinated by the painting, by what the artist has done; he has not tried to create an illusion, to persuade you that this is a real woman, but to make a comment on real women in terms of paint laid on to canvas. Similarly, the theatre is endeavouring to make a comment on real life by symbolical re-enactments of real life, but not to create illusion. This, I think, is coming rather near to Coleridge's definition of imagination. But it seems to me that the suspension of disbelief is essentially a cold and intellectual phrase applying to what is essentially a warm and unintellectual experience. If you want to be intellectual you don't go to the theatre. You do not go to the theatre to have intellectual ideas presented. I know there is something called intellectual theatre, but to me it is a great big crashing pretentious bore. Anybody who has got any sense knows that when human beings get together in large numbers a great performer will fuse their identity; each single person ceases to be himself and becomes a tiny bit of a single collective personality, that of the audience. And the actor's art is to fuse them together, and to play on that great single collective personality. But let nobody fool himself that that collective monster is an intellectual thing! It is a great big mutton-headed baby, very easy to move to laughter, and easier still to move to tears. The most unlikely people in the theatre will die laughing at vulgar jokes. I have seen an archdeacon kicking his gaiters in the air. And the same sort of people, when they think that nobody's looking in the darkness and when they fuse their own personality with that of the crowd, weep unashamedly and healthily and splendidly at the fictitious woes of a King Lear and (God save the mark) at the fictitious woes of the elder Miss Blossom. The stuff doesn't have to be good to make people shed tears. The easy tear is shed at the sentimental rubbish, as we all know from the movies. But this isn't an intellectual experience, so that to speak of the suspension of disbelief is judging chalk as if it were cheese.

Well now, I hope that you have seen, without my having to stress it, where my own sympathy lies; perhaps because of that, indeed I think almost entirely because of that, where I honestly suppose the theatre is tending. It is perfectly clear that the theatre must be tending away from realism. Painting realized by 1860, when Daguerre first got cracking, that the death-knell had sounded for *trompe l'œil*; as soon as photography was established there was no point at all in artists trying to make a faithful representation of an object. What they must do is to make, in some kind or another, an interpretation of it, a comment upon it. Most thoughtful theatre people realized the moment the movies had passed the bioscope stage, that the death-knell was ringing for theatrical realism. But there is a great difference between theatre and painting. The theatre is a collective art. The theatre must move at the pace of the mutton-headed monster, who moves very slowly. Naturalism is still the fashionable and dominant mode in the theatre. In the West End of London in any season, of the plays that are given, I should say six out of ten were still naturalistic representations of lovely drawing-rooms with charming hostesses and elegant curtains; but twenty years ago nine out of ten would have been like that. It is significant that all the more important of the younger writers in one way or another are trying to break out of the naturalistic box. Some of them, like Pinter, still make use of naturalistic scenery, but their dialogue has ceased to be a naturalistic reproduction of conversation. Others are trying to get away from the naturalistic scene.

I think that most of the forward-looking directors are trying to get away from the proscenium, not entirely because of the break with naturalism. Certainly, in my own case, the dominant consideration is the great advance in the intimacy, the fact that by bending the rows and getting them round an open stage you can get so many people close to the actors. It is my belief that the single most serious ailment of the live theatre, in our country, is the fact that unless you can pay very heavily for the best seats, you just don't see enough of the actors. We have all become accustomed to looking at films and to seeing on great Todd A-O screens faces the size of ten-acre fields, each one of their teeth as big as a postcard, and we just don't want any longer to look at minuscule peanuts gesticulating in a big theatre. We want to get close and see what is going on.

3

Unusual Forms of Stage

RICHARD SOUTHERN

I F an individual begins to address a group of people by means of speech, the shape of the crowd that assembles to hear him is generally a crescent. If the individual, instead of speaking, performs some action such as a dance, then the shape of the crowd is more likely to be circular—it encircles the performer. And if two (or more) persons address a crowd, not

FIG. 2. . . . the shape of the crowd is a crescent

by speaking directly to it, but by speaking to each other, i.e. by dialogue, then the shape of the audience may possibly be again a circle. On the other hand if an 'interplay' between two or more performers, whether it is in speech or movement, is associated in some way with a *background* (such as a hut or screen from which entrances are made) then the shape of the audience may, of course, very likely tend towards the crescent again.

48

Fig. 3. *left:*
. . . encircles the
performer

below:
. . . a hut from
which entrances
are made

R.S.

Fig. 4. . . . he must act towards another
player, inwards

Further, if the performance is small in scale and the audience
few in number, both the audience and the actors may be quite
content to be on the flat ground. But if the show becomes
elaborate or the audience large, then some sort of *staging* must
be built to accommodate the one or the other.

In one of the most primitive survivals of a play in Britain,
the Mummers' Play at Marshfield in Gloucestershire, the seven
performers stand in a circle on the open market-place or street
crossing, and neither they nor the audience are on raised
stages.

But for a big audience the players at any rate must be raised.
We find an arrangement similar to Marshfield, but on a vastly
extended scale, in Cornwall and in Lincolnshire for the great
fifteenth-century Moralities. We find an audience thronging a
circle, a circle surrounded by a ring-mound of earth, or by
stands, so that the people can sit aloft, and watch the players
performing in the centre of this circle. But something else was
added essential to the next step in theatre; where those seven
primitive players had stationed themselves round the circle,

they now built a number of tall scaffold-stages. There may have been less or more than seven according to the performance. Each scaffold would have a curtain in front of it and this could be closed. When the curtain opened the player then rose from his seat upon the scaffold and stood there. You see what a new atmosphere is created in theatre; here, in this vast concourse of people a raised player, eight feet above the ground, suddenly says 'I am Solomon,' and they turn to watch him. Now he can dominate as many as a thousand or more people in the open air. He can descend from this scaffold (and he did in fact turn round and by means of a ladder climb down), and then walk through the people on the ground and join another player from another scaffold. And they can act a piece of concerted business, a fight or a discussion or what you will, in the centre of the audience.

There seems to be a consequence depending on this style of acting—I would not press it too much; but I offer for your consideration the idea that when a player comes forward into the centre of a circle, he must act towards another player, *inwards*: the audience watches from outside. But when he is speaking from a raised platform he is acting *outwards*—down and directly to the people, and he then must take a different style of delivery altogether.

This is, then, the great final development in the line, which I have just drawn—namely, from the simple beginning to the elaborate circle, and then a circle to which raised scaffolds are added; next, that hint of a raised stage leads to the first formalized arrangement of something to act on, a stage designed purely for acting. And the first shape that it took seems to have been a fairly high platform. (When I say fairly high, I mean something about five or six feet high, so that a standing audience could look up.) Thus we have the raised player speaking to the people and dominating from the stage.

But to that raised scaffold there was added a certain technical feature which, when it was properly arranged, would allow any kind of play, right up to the most elaborate plays of the Elizabethan period, to be acted without any difficulty or hold-up at all. (With, perhaps, two reservations: for both traps and flying effects are difficult on simple stages.) This arrangement at the back of this stage consisted of two poles and a cross-piece.

FIG. 5. Sketch of a booth stage

You hang a curtain on the cross-piece and thus create three entrances, for a player can enter round either end of the curtains, and he can make an entrance of a special sort through the centre. Behind, there is provided a property room and a dressing room. Finally—the one last feature which is missing here and which you would find on a fully developed Elizabethan stage—they poked up, above the back wall of the curtain, a ladder so that a player could now mount and play a scene as from a window or a wall-top down on to the stage. Simple and primitive as it seems this arrangement was used in England, Flanders, Italy, France, Germany and probably Ancient Greece. It becomes an almost universal formula for non-scenic stage performances.

When the players in the Tudor period began to play indoors,

when they visited feasts (lords' birthdays and wedding feasts and so forth) they performed in a hall. The halls were generally arranged in a standard fashion. At one end there was a dais upon which the lord's table was set, and where the lord and his family sat—a door from the private rooms provided an entrance to the dais. The retainers of the family sat at tables on either side of the hall. The far end of the hall was marked by a particular arrangement: in the side walls there were two doors of entrance, one from the outside world and the other leading through into the back orchard or court; both communicating with the open air. Further, in the end wall there was a door into the kitchen; from it the servants brought the food to the tables. But you can very well understand that to feed here, with the wind and the snow coming in from side doors, or where you can hear and see the preparations in the kitchen, was not ideal. And so screens were built; they consisted generally of two sections either side and one in the centre, thus leaving two openings. Perhaps in many cases this entry was covered and floored over to provide a balcony above. That was the standard arrangement for a hall.

One of the most puzzling irregularities in the history of the theatre comes about this time. Just when the Elizabethan playhouse, with its direct but very developed acting technique, had risen to the top of its ability to hold an audience—when even in a small place like London (as it was at that time) there were four theatres running simultaneously, seating at least, according to records, 2,000 people each—something entirely new came into the British theatre from abroad.

Just when our playwrights were producing with grace and facility a body of plays which we class among the greatest drama of the world, at that precise time, the whole system was swept away by a new movement, a fascinating new fashion coming from Italy. In essence the new scheme was this: upon a stage there was built an arrangement of ingenuity and charm —conceived always by architects or by painters, never by men of the theatre, never by playwrights, never by actors—an arrangement of *scenery*, an arrangement which originally *did not change* with the changing shows. It was put up by an architect and it remained, no matter what show was performed in front of it. One of those sets of scenery is in existence today in

Vicenza, Italy, at the Teatro Olimpico. It is a wonderful architectural confection of building and painting, to suit any play. It was obviously a dangerous new toy—this toy of scenery; it might become boring. And in plays, indeed, it was soon felt desirable to have a change between the acts, and thus the *intermedium* arose. The early plays of the Italian renaissance had, interweaved between the acts, certain extraneous sketches, ballets or what you will, called *intermedii*. And for these the scenery *was* changed. Thus, we find that on such a stage there would first be built houses which represented the fixed architectural setting for the plays and which the architects put up; then, in addition, sliding in between, would come the new pieces of scenery whose purpose was to change the scene for the *intermedium*. For fifty years, or a hundred years, no one was quite happy about how to change these scenes. It was a matter of technical difficulty. Then they invented a device (which, however, we never adopted in England) by which a series of frames went down underneath the stage, each running on wheels on a track below. The changeable scenes were hung on these frames and so could be pulled on and off and made to appear or disappear. And some considerable time later it occurred to the users of the theatre to change the scenery to *suit the place where the play-scenes* were supposed to occur as well as changing the intermedium scenes. In other words, to present you with scenery which set your play. (But all the same, that had not been the original intention of scenery.)

What did other countries do about this idea of scenery? Japan is an excellent case in point. Japan introduced scenery into its popular theatre about the seventeenth century, developed it in the eighteenth century, and invented a revolving stage. Today Japan has given us, in the Kabuki theatre, a delicious handling of the problem of scenery; wide—an almost magnascope wide-screen type of stage—quick changes of scenery, elaborate, exciting; conventional and yet realistic at the same time by some strange achievement of genius. But another side of the Japanese theatre, the classical theatre, would not touch the idea at all, and has developed another form of stage for quite a different purpose with no scenery at all. And it is of some interest to glance at this other non-scenic side of Japanese theatre—the Noh theatre (see Fig. 5). It was similar to

FIG. 6. The Noh theatre

the Elizabethan theatre. The development in Japan from a circular theatre to a conventional raised stage is so parallel to the development in Britain from a circular acting area to a raised stage of very much the same sort, that it makes one wonder whether the essential development of the theatre is not very much the same in all countries of the world.

Now, in recapitulation: that development starts with the simple, ritual performance to a small audience given on the ordinary ground, without any particular preparation. If the audience grows a little it may be good to bank-up the auditorium, so that one has a saucer-shaped arrangement round a sunk centre. It helps the concentration.

Then it would seem that the next step is the development in size of the audience. The theatre becomes popular; several hundred people have to be accommodated. It is difficult to accommodate many people (that is to say 800 or 1,000) in a theatre of that shape. It *is* possible to take on an audience of that size if the player begins to be raised, but not if he is on the flat. Hence, I would submit, comes the invention and the use of the raised stage. It generally has to have behind it a background; it is not common to find a raised stage in the centre of a circle (the early Japanese Noh stage is fairly unusual in this respect). The introduction of scenery now brings us to the last form of stage; in order to hide the machinery needed for scene changes, our raised platform has a frame added at the top and at the sides of the scenery to mask the off-stage. Within that frame the actor is now placed, making thereby a sort of living picture, and you have the 'proscenium arch'.

Of course, at this point it might be delicious to take sides and say that one of those methods is far better than the other. But at this moment there is no chance, and no point in doing that. In all forms of stage the most tip-top work of theatre has been done. In Balinese theatre—dancing that has never been surpassed, costumes and masks that have never been beaten; the Elizabethan Theatre with its drama; the medieval theatre in the round with its superb moralities; the Japanese Theatre with its superb Noh; and, of course, the picture-frame theatre with its scenery—and the great problems which are raised for a playwright when he has to limit himself to using the scenery.

I would finish with a simple point. All of this matter is really simple, it appears complicated at first before one studies it; but with study it resolves itself into nothing one need worry about. You can present an admirable show on a picture-frame stage; though it must be admitted that illusion may sometimes reach the point where one forgets one is looking at a stage, and thinks that one is looking at a picture come to life. Curiously, it is about this matter that people begin to take sides. Some of them find that the attempt to make the stage look like something else, namely a picture come to life, is not the function they would like to see the stage perform. They have said that they would like to see the stage remain a stage with an actor upon it remaining an actor. Who is right? There is no possibility whatever of making a decision. There is no doubt a possibility for personal preference; but above all there is, in my view, a very good case to be made out for keeping one's mind clear for understanding *both* forms of stage, and not confusing them, knowing that one kind of stage can take many shapes, another kind of stage be used in many ways. The only plea that I have is for using these forms of stage with understanding, and not presenting upon one type of stage a show which is far better worked on a stage of another type. Never mix your drinks in the theatre.

4

The Shape of the Theatre

SEAN KENNY

I SUPPOSE the best way to begin is by talking about communication. I think that the least I say about the theatre would be the best. I shall try to go to the beginning, to see how we communicate at all; how we talk to people; how, if you are an artist of some kind, you communicate your ideas. Communication begins with a symbol; it is a piece of colour, or a word, or a note of music, or practically anything that can have a common meaning. I would like to tell you just a short, short story about how one can say something through symbols, say something beautiful through symbols— and the symbols themselves can be beautiful, which is the final quality of art. A couple of years ago I was up in Alaska, Northern Canada, where the Eskimos live. They are practically all fishermen, and do a little bit of farming, not very much. They have four months of summer and eight months of winter. Now a winter of eight months is a long time, especially if you are sitting inside an igloo. And after a time in the igloo conversation runs out. There is very little you can say to your family; you have said all the exciting things that you wanted to say, and the unexciting things. But these fishermen take into their igloos short tusks of polar bears and seals and so on. And they sit crosslegged. And after the conversation runs out they begin to work on these small tusks, measuring about a foot. They use very small tools and work very close to the body. They begin to carve. And they carve little figures, no higher than a few inches, of a mother and child, a fisherman spearing a seal; lots of things. Some things funny and some things sad. Now their symbol is here. I could give two of these things to someone, from my hand. And I would be saying something to them. Maybe it would be funny, maybe sad; but I would be saying something. And the symbols I am using are beautiful as well. Here is an art really (one never knows what it is—the artist always likes to think of it as his job; he is certainly not a special kind of person; it is a job). But this is marvellous, because you have these small figures and they can become symbols of a beautiful expression. I think the craftsman is the man who learns to use the symbol. He learns to use whatever medium he is going to speak through; he learns about it, he learns how to speak through it. And the artist is the man who has something to say through that medium. The sort of jugglers we have today, the Ionescos and the modern painters who ride cycles on canvases, these jugglers are so fascinated by the arrangement of the symbol that they make no effort to speak through them and beyond them. They think it is enough to arrange an interesting pattern. And in literature it is much the same. So we come to this old-fashioned business called the 'theatre'.

Let us examine our theatre and the rest of the arts. Who sees them in the first place? Who actually goes into a gallery and sees the paintings? Who goes to listen to music? Who reads books? Who goes to the theatre? Very few people; practically nobody. The artist today is a man who is involved in the hobbies of a few patrons. The theatre is a kind of hobby. It is not a live voice. It doesn't say anything which will influence the price of a man's loaf of bread. It won't stop wars; it won't even start wars, and that is easy enough. It is not effective; but neither is painting and neither is sculpture, and certainly least of all is architecture—this is the completest rubbish of all. So when we talk about the arts and what the theatre is going to do, we must know who we are talking to. We must know that although *we* all read theatre magazines, and although we are all so full of theatre (because it is our kind of medium, our kind of symbol) we mustn't forget how small it is. Because until we realize how small it is, we can never raise our voice. And the raising of a voice is the excitement. If you know your symbol, and know your craft—which is the theatre—then you can speak through it.

Let us examine the symbol. Let us examine the baroque stage which the Italians gave to us eighty years ago. It is an architectural convention. We have been given a framework; and we are told, 'This is your frame, you must produce your stuff inside this.' So we have this baroque proscenium, with the angels, flutes, and God knows what around it. And an actor has to act sideways because you can't act any way but sideways. When you design you have to cut out with scissors because people only see it from one side. And when you direct a play you have to direct the designer and the actor to behave flat. Most important of all, what about the writer? Probably the main reason that theatre exists at all is because some man wants to tell us a story, and this is the best way to tell it. Now it is about time that we should free the writer from the old-fashioned misery of this Italian stage. Writers have written for it good plays, so it is important that we have it to show these plays; and certainly writers in the future will write for it. But when we think about theatre, we are actually controlled in our thoughts by this shape. An actor will think about the shape; he won't say so, but he will think in its terms. But there must be another way to do it. There must be other ways.

The first time that I got interested in the theatre was in the west of Ireland, where I was born, in a small fishing village. I was about six or seven, and there was an old woman who lived in the village, and she had a lot of chairs in her kitchen. She lived by herself and she had about sixteen chairs in the kitchen. I couldn't understand why a woman needed sixteen chairs. After a while I began to notice fishermen going into her cottage, into the kitchen. And she was telling stories in this room; just an ordinary flag floor, big fireplace, dresser, furniture and so on. We used to sneak in under the legs of the fishermen and lie on the floor and see this woman tell her story. Now her stage was the big fireplace, the big blackened fireplace. And this woman, with a shawl over her head, told these fantastic stories—always beginning inside the audience; she would take a member of the audience, ask about the grandmother—the grandmother's fine and she saw the priest today; and then she would tell a story about a priest or something like that, but always leading off from the audience. When she became dramatic she would move back to the fireplace, and she would poke up the fire and the flames went up behind her. And she had this shawl over her head. She knew about drama. It was marvellous; because here was a story being told and the audience were sitting just wrapped around her. Sometimes she would stand in the middle of the floor, or sit in the middle on a chair, knitting or something like this, and would start a story. This is where she was clever.

One tries to find out at Chichester, and places like that, how you act on that kind of stage. The different focuses of the actor—how do you control or co-ordinate all the expressions so that each person in the audience is getting as much as everyone else?

Peter Brook told me about going to an old Victorian house outside Hamburg. After the war Germany was full of broken-down theatres, bombed theatres, and big actors, not big in height, but big actors who stand like Japanese wrestlers. And they were walking the streets with nowhere to play. But there was a Victorian house outside Hamburg, and these Germans took Peter there, right up to the top to this room. And in this room there was an area approximately six feet by twelve feet and 200 people were crammed in sitting on ledges, on everything. There were four chairs. And on the four chairs were four actors, sitting, waiting for the story. The story was *Crime and Punishment*. The lighting system was two switches. One switch turned off half the lights and the other turned the rest off. There was a cupboard at one side behind the chairs. Now they told *Crime and Punishment* for four hours. They began with a man getting up, walking towards the audience and saying 'Tonight we are going to tell you the story of *Crime and Punishment*. This old woman was walking down the street,' and so the story began. Just like that. This was theatre.

The minority group that we work for, the people who own theatres at the moment, the people who claim us, the people who pay us, all seem to belong to the one way of doing it—the frame. If you wanted a Picasso, and you said, 'Look, Picasso, here is a frame, paint me a picture,' he would throw you out. He would be right. How can we be excited, how can we do anything new, how can we explode inside this frame? Theatre equals proscenium arch, and that really is all it means today. It doesn't mean a place where you can make anything happen. It doesn't mean a place where a director and a group of actors might come in through a door, and the director would say, 'We have this story—I need twelve virgins on that wall. I need a boy and a woman sitting over here. I need an army to come in up there. And I need an acting area here, in the centre.' Now where can you do this? You can't. There is no place to do it. We haven't designed a place where theatre can begin from a white canvas, from a negative expression. All art must begin

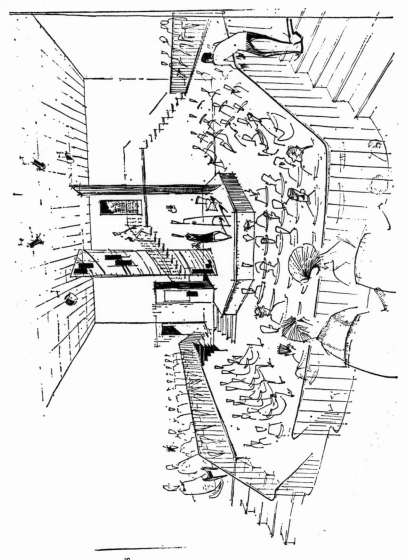

Fig. 7.
Sketch for a
studio with a
movable stage
and many levels
available as
acting areas

from the beginning. It must begin from a nothing beginning. You must forget everything, even things you know, to begin to examine a question. And the examination of a question is what a painting is. If it is a copy, if it's a reproduction of something else, it is stolen and no good. Art has to be an examination. It has to be the artist examining and finding a reason, for, against or whatever. The theatre is the same thing. It is an examination by the writer, with the help of the actors and the director, of something in our life today, something which does affect us vitally, like the price of bread or how wars begin or end, or indeed why people fight at all. But how can we, if we have such an old-fashioned thing? How can we say something brand new?

The theatre doesn't interest the working class because there is nothing exciting in it. They are not excited. They can get excitement on television, and it's very good, There is nothing in theatre which will excite the intellectual. Looking at the theatre he sees adolescent ideas of problems in a miner's hut in Wales, which literature covered a long, long time ago, and so did painting. And yet only today is theatre suddenly coming to the realization that the autobiographical socialist problem is a marvellous thing. Not only, then, are we in our structural form eighty years behind the time, we are also sixty years behind the time in what we do.

Now how do we make progress? We must have hope, as Samuel Beckett says, we must go on. We must go on to something. We must make the theatre alive, an exciting place. It doesn't begin with the architect. It doesn't begin with the frame. It begins as a space, a free space; nothing. It is no good having a National Theatre, a beautiful National Theatre, if you don't have a national theatre company and writers who are going to write marvellous things for it. It begins from the inside and grows in an organic way, like a tree; like anything exciting, like a power station—the design of a turbine and the reason why it is there at all, by that design is the whole design controlled, from the inside. A turbine has working parts, and machinery leads to and from it, and you must have freedom around it. You must be able to reach any part of it. In itself it is very beautiful. From it the outside grows. Theatre happens the opposite way; the outside came first, an old Italian opera

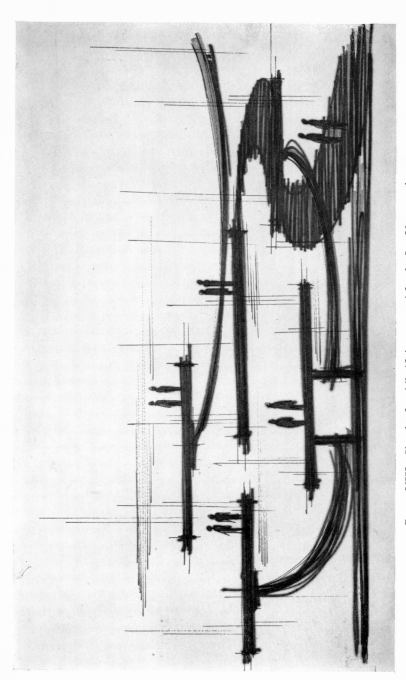

PLATE VIII. Sketch of mobile 'flying saucers' for the Las Vegas project

PLATE IX. The Casino de Paris stage in action at Las Vegas

Photograph by Phil Stern

stage—really that's what it is. It is a disgrace if we continue building those arbitrary stages. Let's have one, surely. But for every one let us have ten barns with nothing inside, so that we can walk in one day and say 'We want a piece of rostrum over there, and a piece over here' and so on.

I had a marvellous thing happen to me. It might be possible for me to do something like this, as well as I can. I have got a studio in Soho, London. About three months ago the door banged wide open and in walked six Texans, with boots and sunburn, close-shaven. And they said, 'are you so and so?' and I didn't deny it; and they said, 'you are going to design our new theatre in Las Vegas', so I said, 'all right'. I couldn't really refuse because there was no discussion. They hadn't come to talk to me about it. They had come to tell me; 'we have flown over the North Pole today to see you, you must fly back with us over the North Pole tomorrow', or words to that effect. 'Now,' I said, 'wait a minute. I can't do that.' But I did go, though not the following day. I went to Las Vegas. It is the most unreal strip of neon light in the desert you have ever seen. It is only a strip of neon light in the desert and nothing else. It is designed for gambling. Purely for gambling. And any attraction in it (theatre included) is to create traffic around gambling tables. It is the last stand of the music hall. And every time I talked to them about the theatre, they kept saying that the Casino had to be arranged directly opposite the front doors of the theatre so that nobody could get to the theatre, even to be turned away, without walking past the gambling tables. However, it is not a joke. They had great confidence in me, and when I eventually got them down to details I had in them too. They want me to do a show for 1963 in the existing theatre, which is a great cabaret hall—a room roughly fan-shaped with a fairly big stage. A show for 1963 and then in 1964 the new theatre begins. The shows there are just legs, ostrich feathers and elevators. That's all. I think ostrich feathers are enough. For the show next year I thought I would get away from chorus line movement. So I began to think about a free space. First of all I began to plan the theatre for 1964. From there I would go back to the stage show for 1963. I thought about spaces which could give you any form you wanted, but flexibly, and very easily. Eventually it came out like a flying saucer. It wasn't intentional, but I found that circular discs were easier to move.

II

What about the painter and what about the musician? Haven't they got something marvellous to give us? It would be good if our theatres had the help of the artists who paint and who write music because they would make our voice stronger. Instead of walking in isolation—a sculptor over there, and a painter here, and there a musician—we should come together in the same place. So you have the idea of a cultural centre. That is all right. But we need these places first in Universities and schools. We need experimental places, experimental spaces, so that we can explore them. You must first sow seeds. Then the tree grows. And beware that you don't sell the fruit until the tree is grown. If you try to give painting and music to the working classes, God help them! If you try to give them music and painting as they are now then that's a cheap culture—it is giving something which is bad and would put people off painting and music for the rest of their lives. This we must beware of. First we must have experimental places. We must have a space, so that we can all come and examine theatre. How do we get these places? Las Vegas is music hall; it is not really theatre. We need a place where something exciting could happen, and it must not be held away from the audience. Now suppose you went into a restaurant and a waiter dropped a tray, and everybody looked around; the manager came out and fired him, and he shot the manager. Suddenly we have a story going. We have theatre. And people go home and talk about it, and say something extraordinary happened at the restaurant last night. A place where we can rehearse (because nothing good is accidental like that), a place where we can take a story and rehearse and work it. But please, please, an open beginning.

If Stephen Joseph wants to have a marvellously designed theatre in the round it's impossible. He has to compromise. He has to use a broken-down cinema. It's not right; because theatre in the round is one way of telling a story; and certainly a good way. So is Chichester. So is the proscenium a good way of telling a story; but it is not the only way. And it mustn't control all our directors, and it mustn't frighten away writers who want to write scenario style. All we get is the writers of adolescent stuff. We don't get a really exciting broad-visioned novelist who could write something like *Crime and Punishment*. He would never come to our theatre to work for us, because he couldn't work in the frame that is all we can give him. It is not jumping far to say this is not right. It would be arrogant to say that any type of theatre is right. But theatre must be free enough so that we can attract the writer, so that we can make it exciting to actors and directors, and most of all to the audiences. The audience, after all, are the second actor, and we must make them excited not only by what is happening but by the way they see it; by their arrangement as well as the stage arrangement. To sit in row M, seat number 7, and be stuck with that point of view all night is very bad. Even if nothing else, theatre in the round, and amphitheatre, could be justified on the grounds of *lets look at the cardboard sideways*. It would be enough. Let us get another point of view to the theatre, and not this medieval church design.

We must not get carried away by the excitement of acclaim. Critics are dangerous people. The critic will acclaim the young writer who writes a first play. And he will kill the writer forever; because he will use the word 'genius'. How can the writer write with that cloud on his head? It's impossible. Most of our young writers in the theatre today are very good; and most of the writers with adolescent ideas are good, but they are in training. They are only in training. They are not full theatre writers yet. And when they are full theatre writers they will either leave the theatre and write a film script, or they become something else. They will become directors. We have to offer them more.

Architects are responsible. The architect must not be so arrogant about the theatre. It doesn't belong to him. Does the architect tell a housewife how she must behave in her own kitchen? Surely he comes to the housewife and says where do you want the sink, where do you want the cooker? And she will say. So with the theatre. The theatre technicians, the actors must say, this is what we want to begin with—a flexible space, or theatre in the round, or a stage at the side. A new building will follow. But the architect must not come first.

5

Theatre and Youth

HUGH HUNT

OUR social conscience today is somewhat over-burdened with the care of youth. Sometimes we may wonder whether greater care should not be given to the old, or even, speaking personally, to the middle-aged. But there is one very practical reason why the theatre should be looking at youth today; not only must it have an audience, but if it is to compete successfully with other media of entertainment, either as private enterprise or as a publicly owned service, it must have a larger audience than it is at present attracting. The theatre audience in this country is not only not large enough, but it is not young enough. It is no use imagining that by the time a man or woman reaches the age of thirty, without discovering the theatre, he or she is suddenly going to see the light. So the theatre, if it is to survive, must attract a larger audience, and quite clearly that audience has got to be found amongst young people.

The question is asked in the Brains Trust (Appendix 2), 'Why should the theatre survive?' Perhaps it isn't answered as convincingly as we would like. I would suggest that it isn't good enough to say that theatre is a great historical asset, nor that because we've always had a theatre we must therefore always have one, nor is it enough to say it will survive because it is a great art. Great arts, like great religions, can die if there is no need for them. The theatre has the right to survive only if it can continue to provide an essential human need. What need can theatres supply today?

We live in an age of science, an age which is dominated by technological development and our lives are increasingly governed by technicians and statisticians. The ordinary man, like you and me, seems less and less able to participate in the creation of anything; for everything seems to be provided for us, and we are often quite unable to understand the machinery which governs us. Machines have taken the place of craftsmanship, statistics have taken the place of thought. We can no longer think out a problem for ourselves and expect to arrive at an answer equal to that provided by a computer. All our arguments have now to be based on statistical research, and synthetic creation has taken the place of much of our original creation. We no longer play music in our homes; we play it on records. We no longer read aloud; we watch television. We no longer go to watch sport; we prefer to see it on television. Wherever we look, there is a decline in active social participation. More and more it is the specialist and his machine which makes the vital contribution. The result is that we seem to have lost our purpose as creative creatures. Instead we have become spectators of life. We don't seem to know what we're here for; except to await the event, whatever that may be.

Many of us feel increasingly isolated from society and we live in little worlds of our own, specializing in our own particular little subject, often failing to communicate with each other, and less and less do we join in a fully developed community life; the sort of life which has hitherto always cemented us into a community. The greatest and most serious loss of our age is the loss of religion. For many of us science with its discoveries has suspended our participation in the old rituals of religion, and communal religious participation was the cement which held our society together and gave us a clearly defined purpose for being born, for living and for dying. The emphasis on technological development is therefore likely to make us lose sight of broad human values. We have lost our sense of communal purpose; we are losing our sense of the values of life itself. But art, which is a kind of religion, or at least an expression of it, has the possibility of preserving these values. And surely no art more so than the theatre; not only because the theatre is a bringing together or meeting place of the other arts, but because it is also the most understandable and most easily recognizable to the common man. There are many of us who find it difficult to appreciate poetry, painting and music, but most of us can appreciate the theatre which comes to us in a human form and is provided for us by human beings. The fact that the theatre is the most easily understandable art, and that it can give us a sense of human values and allow us to participate creatively in a performance, is of the utmost importance in this particular age in which we live. It is of particular importance to young people since its humanist nature can provide a necessary balance to an overdose of technology.

What kind of theatre, then, must we create for the larger and younger audience we must attract if theatre is to survive and serve this essential human need—the need to participate? Good theatre depends on three things: the quality of its repertoire, the quality of its performance, and the quality of its housing; but theatre doesn't only depend on the playwright, the actor and the architect, it also depends on the quality of the audience. The playwright, the actor and the architect are vital factors in creating the quality of theatre, but its survival depends on the extent of the demand. What preparations are we making for meeting and encouraging that demand? Are we, in fact, making any preparations at all for encouraging appreciation of quality in the theatre—quality of plays, quality of performance and quality of the housing in which the performance takes place? We are spending approximately £200,000,000 a year on developing appreciation for the arts amongst our children. That money of course is not wholly being spent on teaching the young to appreciate good theatre as such, but since the theatre is a synthesis of all the arts inevitably any appreciation of the general arts is creating an appreciation of the arts that make up good theatre. As a result of the emphasis we are placing on appreciation of the arts we are likely to encourage more young people to demand a higher quality of plays, of performance, and of aesthetic surroundings than the type of theatrical entertainment and theatre building offered to young people in the past. Can we see any signs of this happening? I think we can.

If you remember the type of plays that were being performed thirty or forty years ago in most of the theatres in this country you will agree that they were, by and large, light entertainments of a post-prandial kind. Light entertainment and thrillers were the most popular fare, though there were, of course, serious plays as well. But serious plays had such minute audiences that they usually had to be housed in club theatres or small theatres patronized by the few. Today the situation has changed. Most of the plays that are written and patronized today are very different from the old drawing-room comedies and thrillers; they are plays with a serious purpose; and when they are comedies, by such writers as Simpson or Pinter, they are comedies which reflect our society and its problems in a satirical and thought-provoking manner, rather than escapist comedies about high society in the South of France or about the comparatively rarefied society of the country house. On the whole the new plays that are being written are plays vitally concerned with life as we live it and of the often terrifying problems we have to face. And these plays are not merely being performed in the coterie theatres which housed most of the serious drama before the war, they are being performed in the commercial theatres and in the civic repertory theatres. In the old days it was almost impossible for an Auden or an Isherwood, or even an Eliot, to break through on to the commercial or popular stage; today there is no recognizable division between the *avant-garde* playwright and the popular playwright. Wesker, Ionesco or Pinter are just as likely to score a popular success as Peter Shaffer, Noël Coward or Terence Rattigan.

To take another aspect of our theatres' repertoire: if you look at the playbills at the Old Vic, Sadler's Wells, Covent Garden, Stratford or the Aldwych, you will find that there are far more classical plays being presented today than ever before. In the pre-war theatre productions of the classics, unless they were studded with stars, had to be put together in the Waterloo Road out of any old odds and ends that happened to be lying around; today they can be mounted magnificently—though not always, of course—and we can see regular seasons of classics, in London and Stratford, as well as in many of the provincial cities. We have regular seasons of opera and ballet, whereas before the war there were no such things as the Royal Ballet nor indeed the Royal Opera Company.

In performance too there has been an improvement. I don't say that we have greater actors today than there were twenty or thirty years ago, but we have, I think, more educated actors. In fact we now educate our actors, which we never did before. The formation of ensemble companies is beginning. Much more care and thought and time are put into rehearsals and preparation for a play than they were in the past.

You may say that most of this change concerns the London theatre. What is happening to the provinces?

There are two types of provincial theatre: the touring theatre and the repertory theatre. The touring theatre is, of course, not strictly provincial in origin; it is controlled by the London managements who mainly use it to try out their plays before they go into London. It is a type of theatre that is gradually disappearing. Fewer and fewer plays are toured extensively before they go into London; many are tried out in the repertory companies, or at Stratford East, or at the Bristol Old Vic, or at the Oxford Playhouse. The pre-London touring theatre is gradually becoming extinct. The post-London tour too has almost entirely disappeared because leading actors no longer need to tour for their livelihood, finding a more lucrative field of employment in television or the cinema. Without leading actors the touring theatre with its increasing expenses is uneconomic. I believe that in about ten years' time there will be practically no touring companies as we knew them in the past. With the exception of such companies as the National Theatre, or the opera and ballet companies which are heavily subsidized, commercial tours from London will no longer be possible. Therefore the whole future of our theatre is going to depend on the repertory theatres. Can the repertory theatres provide the required quality of plays, of performance and of housing to attract sufficiently large audiences to justify the ever increasing financial subsidies they will require?

It is inevitably to some extent a question of finance. The repertory theatres will say they could provide a higher quality repertoire but—except for a few larger repertories—they are not receiving large enough subsidies to present big-scale plays, experimental plays or plays by new and untried playwrights, and consequently their repertoire is limited. They say too that they could attract better actors and directors if they had more money. This is probably true as a generalization, though eventually popular success must depend on the imagination, initiative and determination of the people who run them. Subsidies are, however, being constantly increased, and although the process of persuading the Treasury as well as local authorities that theatres must be properly housed and capitalized if they are to develop their business and perform a worthwhile

function, is deplorably slow, the economic future is not unhope-
ful. Very roughly, we provide at present through the Arts
Council £222,000 every year for the theatre. This may seem a
big sum, but of course it is minute compared with the subsidies
available in most continental countries, which are, as a result,
able to give better service and are consequently attracting
bigger audiences. Out of this total expenditure of £222,000,
£92,000 is being spent on theatres in London, though a great
deal more than this will be spent from next year onwards on the
National Theatre. Most of the big provincial cities—Birmingham, Coventry, Bristol, Nottingham, Oxford—are, however,
receiving a fair share and the present distribution of funds
between the Metropolis and the provinces would seem to be
reasonable; but what worries me is the position here in the north
in relation to the rest of England. For the whole of Lancashire—
the whole of this packed population in the north-west of England, one of the biggest if not the biggest population mass in the
country—only £1,000 is at present being spent on one theatre
—the Oldham Repertory Company—though, it is hoped that
some funds will soon be made available to the Liverpool Playhouse. Is this a proper division of money? And if not who is to
blame? Should we blame the Arts Council? The Arts Council
can only help those who help themselves. The onus of supplying
new theatres and the initiative to form good repertory companies
lies on the shoulders of local authorities, of local institutions and
eventually of each one of us. I suggest that the failure to develop
theatres in the North is one of the reasons why so many young
people find life in this part of England unattractive, and why
it is often difficult for business houses and industries to attract
intelligent young people to move northwards for their livelihood.

The existence of a creative and lively repertory company
which is attracting new playwrights to write for it and good
actors to play for it has far wider implications than the statistics
of the box office would suggest. Just as Bolton is proud of its
Wanderers, though not everyone may go to see them play, so
too might this city be proud of its theatre—of the plays that
could emanate from it and of the actors to whom it could give
birth. In this age of mechanized production and standardized
products in which we as human beings appear to make so little
creative contribution, the theatre—our own civic theatre—

offers us a cause to support, an ideal to aim at, something of human value to which we can, if we wish, contribute, and above all a means of communion with each other. And sometimes— just sometimes—it can give us a glimpse of something greater than ourselves—the purpose for which we were created.

But now let us turn to the more mundane topic of what sort of theatres we should build. First let us consider the site. I have great admiration for the work of the Library Theatre in Manchester; I think it is doing a wonderful job; but I don't believe theatres ought to be tucked down in the basements of libraries any more than I consider they should be fitted into office blocks or luxury hotels as a property speculator's sop to his conscience. The theatre has a right to an existence of its own. It has a right to stand firmly and squarely in the centre of the city as a monument to the imagination and initiative of its citizens; above all it should stand in a place where it can be seen. For theatres must not only exist, they must be seen to exist. Second only to the importance of the site and status of a theatre are the facilities it contains to make theatre-going an exciting and civilized event. We must build theatres where the audiences can move freely in the intervals, where they can feel a sense of their importance as human beings, where they can for a short time forget the drab procedure of standing in bus queues and waiting for tea in the factory canteen. The seating arrangements in the auditorium must no longer be arranged so as to emphasize social differences, starting up in the gallery and working down to the stalls. This social stratification is totally out of date and is, I think, one of the chief reasons why so many of our older theatres have found it hard to attract young people to them. A box office which behaves politely to its patrons and tries to encourage them to go to the theatre instead of treating them as if they were doing the theatre a favour, is surely essential. So are refreshment bars, cloak rooms, restaurants, car parking sites and all the rest of the things that should go with a modern building.

Finally there is the question of the stage, which we have been discussing. Is an open stage necessary? Quite clearly the emphasis in earlier chapters has been strongly on theatre in the round or theatre with an open stage. Are these the only forms in which a theatre should be built? A good deal of scorn has been thrown on the picture-frame stage with its use of illusionist scenery. It is right that the emphasis should have been placed on new forms, but it is, I think, wrong to regard the picture-frame stage as being unable any longer to attract a contemporary audience. The theatre of Jean Vilar in France (The *Théâtre Nationale Populaire*) is a picture-frame stage and, indeed, most continental theatres which have been built since the war and which are successfully attracting large audiences are built in this style. Although a production of Shakespeare may have many advantages on an open stage, it is not the form of the stage which dictates the success of the performance. The Chichester Festival would have been no less successful if it had been housed in a modern theatre with a picture-frame stage. I don't believe the production of *King Lear* at the Aldwych Theatre would fail to attract crowds of young people to it merely because it is presented on a picture-frame stage. Neither the open stage, theatre in the round nor the picture-frame stage are going to affect the future popularity of the theatre. But at the same time it is right that emphasis should have been placed on the various forms of open stage in this book if only to open our eyes to their possibilities and advantages and to dispel some of the prejudices against them.

Undoubtedly the new forms of open theatre have added, and are adding, great richness to theatre itself. They are providing a new impact of theatre on the public, if only by providing a new talking point, and they are opening up new ways and sweeping away some of the cobwebs that have accumulated round forms that had become too conservative. Any theatre which is built today must take these new forms—or rediscovery of old forms—into account. Young audiences want to discover the theatre for themselves and they want to discover it as something different from the theatre of past generations. They want old truths in new forms. It is not beyond the skill of an architect aided by technologists to devise a form of theatre which can combine the picture-frame, the open stage, the arena, within one building. Even if these forms are not all housed in the same auditorium, the auditoria can at least be placed close enough to each other so that the stages and their amenities can serve each other. Finally, let us remember that theatre brings together the technologist and the artist and that through the medium of new theatre buildings a unique opportunity is now open to technicians to join with actors and architects in preserving and developing the human values which the theatre represents and in helping to create a theatre of a higher quality which alone will meet the needs of a new and demanding young audience.

6

Leisure and the Performing Arts

JOHN ENGLISH

I TOO believe that the future is full of promise for the theatre. We have been saying the theatre is dying now for many many years, and it hasn't died. I don't believe for a moment that it will die. I think we have every reason to be pleased with the standard of work available in the theatre, the standard of writing, the standard of presentation, and the standard of production and acting. But I think we have everything to be ashamed of in the part which the live theatre plays in our life today.

A lot of what I want to say covers a rather broad sociological field, but I hope to take you with me through a certain amount of basic reasoning into a particular scheme which is now being worked out in a rather interesting way, in the Midlands. Our problem there is comparable to the problem in Manchester. I am very familiar with Manchester, and have worked for a number of years in its Library Theatre. Manchester's situation is very like the situation in Birmingham. We too have a vast industrial area all round us.

We are talking about young people in the theatre. How do we interest young people in the theatre, with the hope that as adults they will continue to be interested in the theatre? Can we come to grips with this problem? Well, quite frankly, I think the problem of interesting young people is precisely the same as that of interesting anybody in the theatre. I am going to produce a few statistics. Some of them are rather alarming. Let us consider for a moment how many people at present in our society in our second, third, or fourth generation of compulsory education, at a time of greater affluence and a time of greater and much better physical conditions, of much more money and much more leisure time, how many people are interested in the theatre? And indeed how many people are interested in the performing arts? I think it will help if I consider the theatre, not in isolation, but as one of the social and cultural manifestations of the human spirit. Let us consider the world of the performing arts as a whole and think of the theatre as one part of it; this will be useful.

How many people are interested in the performing arts? We must sweep one or two things to one side for the moment. It is true that there is much participation in events, in the exercise of the imagination, through some form of dramatization; it deluges us from every direction. Most of us experience every day, for many hours of the day, some sort of dramatization. But it may not be anything more ostentatious than twentieth-century folk tales, the one from my part of the world, *The Archers*, and the one from your part of the world, *Z Cars*. This form of (I'm trying not to use the word entertainment) exercising the mind, besides the imagination, has entered into everybody's life. This is a new phenomenon. It is something that didn't exist until twenty or thirty years ago. There is more participation in dramatic entertainment than there has ever been. What about the theatre itself? What about the social art of coming together in a group way, for the group enjoyment of these things? Let me quote you the statistics from my own home region, for Birmingham. Population about the same as here with its surrounding areas. We are lucky in Birmingham. We still have some cultural life left. We have three theatres; one of them is a very famous theatre, the second in the line of repertory theatres to your theatre here, the Gaiety Theatre. We have a splendid provincial orchestra. Some people think that it is better than the Hallé. We have a splendid Art Gallery which, I think, is better than the Walker, Liverpool. We have a host of minor cultural societies of one sort or another. We have quite an extraordinary collection of amateur little theatres. This is pretty good compared with the rest of the country. But what does it amount to? Here come the statistics. If all the seats in all these theatres were full every night, and every seat for every amateur performance, every students' union performance, every choral society, were full on every occasion (and we know this isn't so), if every seat for every city orchestra concert and every chamber music concert were full, and every square yard of the Art Gallery were full day by day—there is still only physically room for 1 per cent of the population that these institutions serve. One in a hundred. Now this is extraordinary. And our institutions are patronized by the same small group of people. We are a very close circle. We enjoy one another's company. So it is in fact less than 1 per cent. Now I suspect your figures are worse than this. In Manchester you have a denser population than we have; we have some country, a lot of arable land, within about ten miles of Birmingham, so we are diluted by rural influences. For the rest of the country it is very much worse. Five hundred theatres have been closed in Great Britain since the end of the last war. Seven or eight new ones have been built.

Here is an even more disturbing statistic. Let us take the Birmingham City Art Gallery. It is housed in a Victorian building, but it has some splendid things inside it. It has been rejuvenated. It has not only our own special collection of pre-Raphaelites, but it has a splendid collection of moderns; not only paintings but sculptures; not only these things but associated pleasantries—china, silverware, jewellery. It has a smashing coffee bar, as nice a place to have coffee as anywhere in the city, and this is much patronized by students and by the public. Last year some 650,000 people went into that gallery. And this sounds quite impressive—just short of three-quarters of a million. But when the gallery opened in 1885 a million and a quarter people went into it. And the numbers remained in the millions until the beginning of the first World War. Then they fell steadily. The numbers have dropped by over thirty thousand in each of the last two years. Remember these figures—a million and a quarter in 1885, less than three-quarters of a million now; and in that time the population that the galleries serve has multiplied by five times. This means that only about a tenth of the people now go into a place, which is a much more pleasant place to be in than it ever was in 1885, to derive aesthetic pleasure and satisfaction and some sort of fulfilment from looking at objects of beauty. It is a very distressing fact indeed. I know you could argue that the poor devils in 1885 probably had not anywhere else to go out of the rain and out of the cold, but into a Public Gallery; but this isn't the whole truth. By and large, people now are not concerned to stir themselves for these things at all. Is this adequate for a healthy society? You can argue that all these things (a want for music, for the theatre, for the visual arts) are a minority interest, that they always will be. I am not at all sure of this. There is not anything particularly remarkable about us. We are very average people. It seems to me that this gift to derive satisfaction and enjoyment from these pleasures is widely broadcast. I am pretty certain that the problem is one of availability and accessibility. We go to the theatre, concerts, and we are interested in pictures because we have been made aware of them, partly through education—but not entirely. If you search back in your past you will probably find that you first went to the theatre, and first went to a concert, because your Mum or your Dad or Grandparents took you there. This is largely a matter of introduction in the right sort of context.

Now I want to give you some more statistics, to put the importance of the problem on the right scale. We are in a rapidly changing world. It is not only a question of physical change. As I came into Manchester I was struck by the similarities of what was happening here to many cities, and in particular Birmingham, where acre upon acre of Victorian cottage dwellings are being swept away. For the first time, for the majority of people, urban areas are being made sensible places in which to live. The upper classes have made a good job of living in towns for centuries, and now, for every Tom, Dick and Harry, living in a town is becoming at least civilized. Our homes are becoming civilized. A great deal of the drudgery has been taken out of everyday life in the home just as it has been in the factory. There is no doubt that our children and our children's children are going to live in a very much more satisfactory physical world than ours.

A word about the time scale of living. We are now living fifteen years longer than we did at the beginning of the century. Not only are we living on average fifteen years longer, which means, on average, our children will live for at least seventy-five years, probably eighty years. There seems no doubt but that we are going to spend longer over our youth. I know that we are maturing more quickly, but let us take youth as the time up to which we are expected to take a major part in keeping civilization going, in keeping the wheels of industry going. My guess is that in fifteen or twenty years' time most people will not begin their serious task in life until the mid-twenties. Even now if you go to a university you don't reckon to start until you are in your twenties. Again, at the other end of the time scale ages of retirement have gone down over the last forty or fifty years. People used not to think of retiring till they were seventy-five, if they lived that long; then seventy, sixty-five, sixty— fifty-five we are hearing of already. My guess is that in fifteen or twenty years' time the age of retirement will come down to something like fifty. This is the sort of pattern then. We are going to live for three-quarters of a century, on the average. The first twenty-five years of our life we shall spend in preparing for our major participation in society. The next twenty-five years we shall spend doing just that. For the last twenty-five years of our life we shall have finished education, we shall have finished our major task in life—what do we do with it? What are we supposed to do with life? Let us consider the middle third of our existence, the middle twenty-five years, our major working efforts. In my lifetime hours of work have gone down from a not uncommon twelve hours a day sometimes seven days a week, to nine and a half hours, eight, and seven. In New York the other day the electricians concluded an agreement for a five-day week, five-hour day. Heads of state to east and west say that the aim of their civilizations is, in fifteen or twenty years' time, for an average of five or six hours' work a day. Consider what this means. For the first time in history, for the majority of mankind, the pattern of the working week will be something like this: two clear days in seven without any work responsibility at all, and on working days five or six hours' work, eight hours' sleep, ten or twelve hours' non-work time, free time, leisure time if you like. Free time for what?

Now this is a completely new circumstance. It has never existed for most people since the beginning of time. All our society has been work orientated. You have got up in the morning, at dawn, and gone out into the fields—later to factories—to scrape a living for your family. You have come home exhausted at night (you slapped a bit of mud on the roof to keep the rain out) and rested briefly, to get up the following morning to work again. Now for the first time within the last thirty to forty years the main interest in life is not work, it is something else. Let me suggest that this something must include leisure. We are already talking about the problems of leisure. This is ironic, isn't it? What do you mean by leisure? I have been talking a great deal about leisure, and looking for a good definition. I haven't found one, but here is a rather interesting and rather charming and pointed definition, from the early eighteenth century, and it goes something like this— *freedom or opportunity to do something*. This is a bit of a shock. We regard leisure as freedom or opportunity to do *nothing*. Young people do regard non-work time, leisure time, as freedom or opportunity to do *something*. Well, to do what? What is the first thing we think of doing with our leisure? Physical recreations, to knock a ball about, to watch other people knocking a ball about; to run, to swim, to ride, to jump, to walk. These are splendid. Man is a physical animal. We must exercise our limbs, and we get all kinds of fulfilments and satisfactions in this way. We have recognized this for many years. Local authorities and everybody else help to provide playing fields, gymnasiums, swimming-pools, for the physical recreations of young people. And the introduction to physical recreation is made in the schools. It is continued as a leisure-time activity. We regard this as being enormously important. It is seen as a normal leisure-time occupation. Well now, to put it no higher than this, is there not a normal sort of play, a different sort of play from the physical recreations, a play of the mind, a play of the spirit, a play of the creative imagination? This to me is the world of the arts. I don't think we have to be any more highfalutin about it than that. This is the world of poetry, of literature, of theatre, of music, painting, of sculpture, of everything that is beautiful for the enhanced experience it can give. We are aware of this. But for most people it is the largest unexplored territory of human behaviour. And it is where a great deal of our time in the future is going to be spent, if we are to fulfil ourselves as human beings. All sorts of ethical, moral and religious questions are tied up with this. But this part of human behaviour must be explored. How are we going to do it?

You say we already possess our theatres, our concert halls, and art galleries. I have shown you how much we value them, and how much they concern people. They concern, by and large, the few offspring of the traditional leisured classes. This is the point, isn't it? Who have been the patrons, throughout history, of the arts? The people who had leisure. It was they who sponsored them, who practised them. They introduced them to their offspring, in their own homes. They supported the theatre and art galleries. We are all, every man Jack of us, the leisured classes now. But we are in a foreign territory. It is territory of which we have had no experience. How do we get in? How do we get from the outside to the inside? If only one in a hundred, or one in two hundred people are interested how do you set about getting more people interested? What are the barriers that stop people from being interested in the theatre, in the arts generally? A certain amount of research work has been done on these questions. A great deal more remains to be done.

A certain amount of *ad hoc* research was done in connection with the Belgrade Theatre at Coventry. With a little money from the Gulbenkian Foundation, enquiries were made amongst young people, young students in the technical colleges, in the senior classes at school, and in factories, shops, and offices, to find out why they didn't go to the theatre. It became apparent at once that they didn't go to the theatre. The reason why they didn't go to the theatre? All sorts of interesting and practical reasons were offered; social reasons, the theatre doesn't belong to us, it is not for the likes of us, it is a middle-class and middle-age sort of thing; we don't know how to behave in the theatre, we feel at a loss, we feel always that somebody is trying to put us at a disadvantage—the lady in the box office, the programme girl; I take my girl to the theatre, I don't know how to behave in the interval, I did not know of the existence of the interval, I don't know what a programme is. Now there is a certain amount of truth in this. But they are nearly all excuses. Certainly people are frightened of penetrating this territory. There is a middle-class culture, and there is a working-class culture. But at the end of the second and third generation of compulsory education culture is accessible to all of us. We haven't woken up to it yet. Now how are you going to make good this gap? How are you going to interest people in the theatre? We have been trying to do this through the Arts Council. Their financial resources do not amount to much anyway. I expect you know that the

Secretary General of the Arts Council has some amusing figures. He points out that the total amount of subsidy to the arts is about a twentieth of the egg subsidy, and a tenth of the tomato subsidy, and half (believe it or not) of the cucumber subsidy. I never knew that a cucumber subsidy existed. But in spite of all the efforts to sustain and nourish the arts, it doesn't work. Five hundred theatres have closed since the existence of the Arts Council. I won't be unkind enough to say this is because of the existence of the Arts Council. But in spite of the Arts Council five hundred theatres have closed. I think we have made the cardinal error of starting at the wrong end. We have started with the old ones, with the middle-aged ones, who should be perfectly well able to look after themselves. I think we have to start at the very beginning. We have to start at the age at which children are subjected to comparable influences on the imagination through the medium of cheap literature, cheap periodicals, radio, television, films. It seems to me elementary that you have to provide for the youngest of children, at the time when they become conscious of the external world. And you must provide them with the very best of experiences in the arts. And you must go on providing these experiences through their time of growing up, at a level of their own understanding, in a way to stretch their understanding, into their young adult life. I try to use the right words. This could sound like a culture factory machine; you put everybody in at one end and make sure they go through the necessary curriculum; this certainly wouldn't work. But at the moment these things are not available at all. If you want your children to be interested in the theatre (except in one or two isolated examples such as the Library Theatre, Manchester, or the Arena Theatre Company) you have to wait years, to pick up the odd crumb from the adult table. I am sure this is not the right way to do it. You must make available experiences in all the arts, in the right sort of context, at the right sort of level.

We are apt to underestimate the sophisticated and conventional nature of these experiences. I don't believe that you automatically recognize something to be good. You don't automatically understand something because it is a work of genius. There is an ABC, a vocabulary, a syntax, and most of all a prosody of the arts to be absorbed into the bloodstream. This takes time. The theatre is a highly conventional experience, a highly conventional art. One may regard oneself as an initiator, but you are in fact building on the shoulders of everyone who has gone before you for two thousand years or more, and your capacity for understanding and enjoyment will depend on the in-built understanding of past conventions and experiences. This is absolutely necessary for a proper understanding of the arts. I don't think that it is hard to come by. I think that in an amazing way the human spirit rises. It would in fact be remarkable if it wasn't so. Works of art are usually the product of a very ordinary simply human people. And they are accessible to us all, provided we have a key to the language, a key to the structure.

I have tried to suggest that the way to create a state of society in which these things are wanted is to make them available at the right sort of standard. Let us be aware that the performing arts will embrace the practising arts, and our own participation in the practising. But let us face up to this; however much we may be interested in the practice of the arts ourselves, we all form the 98 per cent of the audience. Again the words are all wrong. 'The audience' implies sitting back and listening, 'spectators' implies sitting back and watching. This is not true of the live occasion, which can only take place with the willing attention and sympathy and understanding of everybody who is taking part in the occasion. We are 98 per cent of us on most occasions not actors, not musicians, not painters, we are the enjoyers on the other major side of the fence. So this business of getting the ABC and the vocabulary and the syntax and the prosody into our bloodstreams is very much a matter of learning how to enjoy the performing arts. Out of this will grow for every one of us the desire, and the ability, and I hope the opportunity to practise one or other aspect of the arts. This we must provide for as well. I suggest to you that the only way of getting young people and eventually young people when they grow up (this is the whole population) interested in the arts is to provide them with the very best of experiences, from the earliest years. To do this you will need new theatres, new concert halls, new art galleries, dedicated to this purpose. You will also need new studios, new workshops, in which they can practise. Then you will find a new generation of people who can lead others into these new avenues of human experiences.

What kind of theatres do we need? You need all sorts of theatres. If your object is to give us in our bloodstreams a knowledge of the whole of the past background of the theatre so that we can appreciate all illusion and reference and so forth, we must have experience in every sort of theatre since the beginning of time. Our theatres must be capable of presenting plays in a way which will bring the greatest out of them. The theatres and the concert halls that are needed for the new Arts Centres for young people will have to be truly adaptable. They will have to be extremely catholic too. They must contain not only the theatre of the spoken word, they must be suitable for ballet, for opera, for circus even—all manifestations of human endeavour and human artistry when performed in conjunction with other live human beings. I believe in the arena theatre, and I believe in the open stage. But I have been, with our architects and study groups, leaning over backwards to ensure that our open stages and our arena theatres are capable of accommodating a picture-frame stage. This is absolutely necessary, I am quite sure. And I don't think this is difficult.

You may think that I am asking a lot to expect children to be able to acquire a workable background knowledge of what the theatre offers, and what music offers, and what the visual arts offer. I don't think it is difficult at all. I think it is fairly simple provided you learn the rules in a fairly simple sort of way. This conviction is born of our experiences in the Arena Theatre Company where, mainly on the north-east coast, and in south Wales, we have provided since 1948 experiences in theatre of just this classical kind to children from five or six years of age up to their teens. We now have a generation which we have bred ourselves. We find that at fifteen we have audiences who are able to understand and to appreciate Anouilh, Fry, Beckett, Simpson, Pinter, Wesker, Osborne, Sheila Delaney. I believe that the true nature of the theatrical experience can be absorbed and can be understood by children of five or six years of age. Children are very ready to be moved. This is one of the things that we try to do in the theatre. They are very ready to be romantic, and they are very ready to lend sympathy. The idea of the willing suspension of disbelief is not unknown to them. In fact they have spent the previous five years mainly doing just that.

To summarize: the problem of interesting young people in the theatre and in the arts generally is really the problem of interesting all people. The theatre ought to be seen as part of the performing arts as a whole. There is a pressing necessity to open the doors and windows, to introduce these horizons to people in the world of increasing leisure which lies before us. I think there are enormous social implications in doing this, quite apart from our own question of survival. Indeed I think that it is the social implications which are of the greatest importance. Our own satisfaction and enjoyment will follow afterwards. We have to bring about a considerable change of attitude towards the arts. We have two rather unfortunate attitudes towards the arts in this country; in particular we regard art as an improving, do-gooding thing, something that ought to be obviously repelling; this is why we put theatres in the basement, or alongside the town hall. The other unfortunate attitude is to regard the arts as being over-sexual things—not quite nice, something one ought not to indulge in. This is still with us you know. Every girl who gets into a drama school has gone through a struggle with her family before she gets there. Until the enjoyment and practice of things which have a primarily aesthetic value (rather than a physical value) become as natural as breathing, we shall not have won the particular battle which I think it is necessary to fight.

In the Midlands, in addition to the three theatres which we have, we have on the stocks a new civic theatre which will start building within the next four or five years. We have agreed in principle to create a new opera house, a new philharmonic hall, a new chamber music hall, in addition to the facilities that we now have. In preparation for the next fifteen or twenty years we have set up a new independent educational trust with the job, over the next twenty-five years, of trying to produce a culturally literate society, of providing the means whereby young people from five to twenty-five years of age can come to know, in the very best conditions, the satisfactions of music, theatre and the visual arts. To do this we are going to build a large theatre, a truly adaptable theatre, for capacities of from 500 to 2,000 which can take every shape of theatre you can imagine. It must provide for ballet, opera, and music. As well, a small theatre seating 300, suitable in addition for puppetry. A large concert hall and a small concert hall, an art cinema, new type of visual arts gallery, new exhibition hall, arts club with its own studios, library, lecture theatre; all this intermingled with a great many studios and workshops where more and more young people can come to grips themselves with the creative aspects of art. And social facilities—restaurants, coffee bars, an open-air swimming-pool, skating-pool, tennis courts, squash courts. Where is all this going? In the centre of the city? No. It is going somewhere within a mile and a half of the city, somewhere which signals from the beginning that you are supposed to enjoy yourself in a leisure sort of way. This is supposed to provide pleasure. It is going into a public park. The city has laid aside some fifteen acres of its very best park for this purpose. Now this is an enormous advance straight-away. It is opposite the county cricket ground. We hope that in ten years' time we will reach a situation where youngsters will get off the bus to decide whether they will go left into the county cricket ground to see the Australians, or right to go to a performance of the Hallé Orchestra, or to see ballet, or spend a couple of hours in the studio. I have outlined the principles behind all this, but there is a great deal more of practical importance. It is not solely a civic affair. There are some ten or twelve local authorities concerned with this, but there is also the trust, which is made up of the theatres, the orchestras, the amateur societies, all the other cultural bodies, industry, education, everyone from every conceivable grade of religious organization, and youth organization. This is a truly communal affair.

Architects: Powell and Moya, London. Photograph by W. J. Toomey

PLATE X
The stage
of the
Festival
Theatre
at
Chichester

The Chichester
Festival Theatre

CHRISTOPHER STEVENS

THE theatre stands on the edge of a park with its main entrance from the Chichester/Midhurst road. At the south boundary of the site is 'Sloe Fair' which is a City Council car park for 500 cars. There are fine trees on the site, including some magnificent elms. These and all the other trees have been preserved. The Hospital Laundry will be screened from the theatre site by new planting. The main entrances to the theatre are under cover —a canopy being formed by the overhang of the auditorium. The glass doors of the northern half of the foyer open out on to the park. The stage door and the dressing-rooms are on the eastern side of the building.

The main roof is almost flat; the height from its eaves to the ground is 37 feet. The central area of the roof slopes more steeply than the rest, revealing to the observer on the ground that the building is indeed roofed over and not open to the sky.

The auditorium floor is stepped and made of pre-cast reinforced concrete, supported on reinforced concrete beams and columns cast in situ. The enclosing walls which are non-structural, are of special insulating concrete planks. The roof has a clear span of 119 feet and its structural members are all visible from inside. It is supported on a 'cradle' of three tension members each pre-stressed to 140 tons and each consisting of four 1¼-inch diameter high tensile steel rods. These are anchored to the reinforced concrete frame at the top of the six corners of the auditorium and, by their pull on these corners, help carry the overhanging beams supporting the upper seating tiers. A ring beam of latticed steelwork is carried on the cradle and this ring beam in its turn supports the roof covering—a spider's web of light steel and timber joists, covered with wood-wool slabs which have an open-textured finish in areas needing sound absorption and a smoother, harder finish where reflection is required. The roof is waterproofed with three layers of bituminous felt with a gravel finish. Inside, the roof is painted dark blue and grey.

Fresh air is drawn into the auditorium through fans which incorporate electric heaters. The air is drawn out through the open riser on the front step of the stage, along metal trunking to the ventilation plant room and thence to the outside air. The stage lighting and the main house lighting are suspended from a lighting bridge which spans across the centre of the hexagonal roof girder. This girder itself has walkways all the way round so that the central portion of the roof forms a sort of grid, to which access is obtained by means of a Jacob's ladder. Most of the lighting equipment and all the high-level plug boxes are mounted on this grid and it is possible to angle and colour the spotlights between performances from the grid alone without the use of ladders. In addition there are three spot-bars above the stage.

The audience is arranged on three sides of the stage which is placed at one apex of, and contained within, the hexagonal auditorium. The hexagon was chosen in preference to a circle for structural simplicity and economy, and because it is expected to give better acoustics. The upper levels of the stage are made of easily demountable sections and can be rearranged or added to for different productions. The stage flooring is of Canadian maple.

There are nearly 1,400 seats and the most distant are only 60 feet from the stage. Most of them have arms and are upholstered in dark blue. Those in the back rows are upholstered but without arms. The side galleries are not isolated from the rest of the auditorium but form a continuation of the upper tiers. The lighting and stage control box has an uninterrupted view of the stage.

The floor is covered with a dark green nylon carpet. The walls of the auditorium and the three tiers of the stage are painted in varying shades of warm grey.

By raising the auditorium from the ground, the whole of the space underneath it can be used—as an entrance foyer, dressing-rooms, cloakrooms, etc. The supporting skeleton of the building

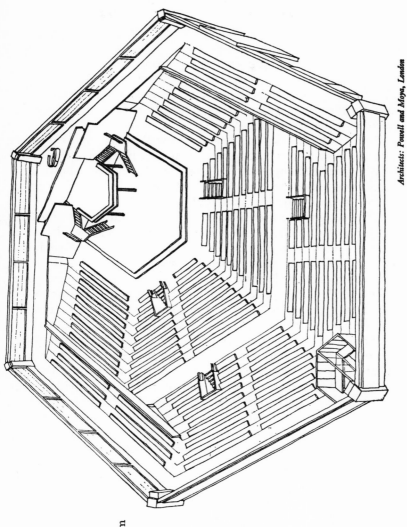

FIG. 8.
Projection
showing the auditorium
and stage of
the Festival Theatre
at Chichester

is exposed and is of reinforced concrete cast on the site and bush-hammered so that its aggregate is exposed. The infilling walls are of lightweight concrete planks painted dark brown. The staircase windows are of wood planks painted white with narrow strips of glass between, giving inside a sense of enclosure and forming a transition between the glass-walled foyer and the windowless auditorium.

Externally the aim has been to express as clearly as possible the internal design and planning of the building—the tiered auditorium encompassing the stage is clearly seen showing its underside raised on supporting columns with glazed-in space below, forming the entrance and foyer.

The design, the first of its kind in this country, is based on a recent movement in favour of the return to the character of the Greek and of the Elizabethan theatres, in which the audience virtually encompassed the players and where the stage was of a more simple nature than the modern proscenium stage. The detailed arrangement of the building has been evolved in collaboration with Sir Tyrone Guthrie and Sir Laurence Olivier.

The building has been paid for by voluntary contributions from the public and the cost had to be kept extremely low. Little money was available for finishes and refinements. To keep initial building costs down, ancillaries normally provided with a theatre have been kept to a minimum. The temporary hutted accommodation for restaurant, administrative offices, scenery, etc., will, it is hoped, soon be replaced by permanent additions to the theatre which has been designed with this in mind. The building contract was for £95,064. During the course of building it was possible to incorporate improvements, due to the promoters' success in raising money, to a value of about £10,000. The lighting installation—largely production lighting —was not included in the building contract and cost about £18,000.

A Brains Trust

HUGH HUNT (*Chairman*):

I am going to start by asking the Brains Trust this question: *Should the art of the theatre be the art of the people or the art of the few?*

STEPHEN JOSEPH:

At the moment it seems to me that the theatre is the art of the few, and I believe that it should be the art of the people. But it should be the art of the people in the sense that it is an art which belongs to people. People should go to theatre and be familiar with its conventions of presentation. They should accept that theatre is an experience they are all going to enjoy. But I don't want theatres to be huge places. I want to see theatres that are small, catering for a popular audience.

DAVID SCASE:

I think theatre should be both popular and for the few. If Stephen Joseph is right in suggesting that we don't want large theatres then the theatre can never be a mass entertainment. The theatre audience must always be a minority with the broadest representation. It belongs to no particular section of the community. We have people from every section and every class coming into the theatre. We need large theatres; but we must also have the experimental theatre.

W. A. DARLINGTON:

Well, unless it is *both* there just isn't a theatre to me.

PERCY CORRY:

Yes, I agree that we must have both. I think it will be many years, many decades, before the theatre is once again a mass medium of entertainment. But we want large theatres for mass entertainment and we want small theatres for selective entertainment. We also want experimental theatres for the people who don't wish anybody to understand it but themselves. It is the cranks that cause the revolutions.

GRENFELL BAINES:

I can't help thinking that if we have a lot more theatres for a few people we should have a lot more jobs for architects, so I should be in favour of theatres for small audiences. It reminds me, though, of a sensitive man who found himself in a large crowd at Charing Cross, and he thought how terrible it must be to belong to the masses. Then it occurred to him that they must have been thinking the same thing about him. And he became one of them right away. So I am for theatre for the people, and I am slightly horrified at those special theatres for the curious few; I would like them to mix now and again with ordinary people.

CHRISTOPHER STEVENS:

Architects might get more jobs if there were more theatres, but there would also be more jobs for actors and producers. More important, if there were more theatres, if people could learn to accept the theatre as an ordinary experience and forget that it is so special or experimental, or so conservative or so expensive or so cheap, if it could be an ordinary everyday thing, this is what we should be working for. I think there is room for the large theatres and for the small theatres.

HUGH HUNT:

The second question:

Shouldn't a theatre be able to pay for itself to justify its existence? Why should the public have to subsidize something in which it appears to have but little interest?

W. A. DARLINGTON:

I believe that the subsidized theatre is the theatre of the future, in the sense that economics have gone to such a point that you just cannot produce a worthwhile play, which appeals to anything but a popular audience, without losing money on it. The only kind of play that can make money now is the play which the larger popular public is going to support. Now and then you do find a very high art production will bring the popular public in, as in the case of *King Lear* at the Aldwych Theatre at present. (The rush for seats for *King Lear* is such that I have had an enormous number of complaints from the public either that they cannot get the Aldwych Theatre on the telephone, or that, when they get there, they are not in time in the queue before the box office closes.) That can happen, but you can't depend upon it, and if we are to have a worthwhile theatre for the future we shall have to pay for it in exactly the the same way as we pay for worthwhile pictures, literature, and all the other things that have been, for generations, provided by the State.

DAVID SCASE:

Let us look at the last part of the question which suggests that the public really isn't interested. Is the public interested in drains? It is not a facetious question. If you took away the drains tomorrow, because the public were not interested, the health of the nation would suffer. Drains are highly subsidized, and I honestly believe that the health of a nation is reflected in the interest it takes in its theatre. If we take away everything that the public isn't keen on paying for, the standard of life we know would disappear completely. The hall we are sitting in, the University itself would disappear. By all means try to make all theatres, particularly civic theatres, pay for themselves as far as possible. But if it means constantly cutting down the scale of production, salaries for the actors, the number of actors you can employ until you reach the level where you can pay for the theatre, then the theatre would diminish to a constant sequence of *Quiet Week-ends* for the next twenty years. We should make it pay when we can. But we should have the right to subsidy, provided that we can guarantee that we shall fill the theatre. Then the subsidy is well worthwhile. I do not believe in subsidizing empty theatres.

STEPHEN JOSEPH:

The question of the distribution of public money is a very vexed one. Don't build the next bomb (and I'm sure no one particularly wants to) and with the money saved you could build 500 theatres in this country and run them without anyone paying for a single ticket for the next fifty years.

GRENFELL BAINES:

I am in complete agreement with the idea that we should make sure some of these worthwhile things are paid for. And possibly the theatre in total could pay for itself by virtue of an entertainment tax. An entertainment tax on bingo, pools and other things could be devoted to helping the theatre proper.

HUGH HUNT:

In Denmark the cinema entertainment tax is devoted to the subsidization of the theatre.

CHRISTOPHER STEVENS:

The thing that disturbs me is the suggestion that a production to be popular has to be expensive. I am quite sure it doesn't. I am quite sure you have to have good actors.

DAVID SCASE:

It is a criminal fact that many times a director in an ordinary provincial rep has to say 'I can't do *The Crucible*, but might do *The Rainmaker* (both good plays perhaps!), because for *The Crucible* twenty actors are needed', and if you need the actors, you must pay the actors. But the point that Mr Baines raised, concerning entertainment as a whole, is important. The repertory theatres already subsidize, by low wages, both I.T.V. and the film industry. The repertory theatres train and develop the actors who, in turn, go to these highly profitable concerns. If profits from I.T.V. and B.B.C. and all the film companies were put together, with the profits from commercial theatre in the country as a whole, of course theatre would pay! If you take the theatre as a whole it pays. But we penalize one small department, which includes the average repertory theatre, and we force it into low wages, and into having comparatively small casts. An actor in a repertory theatre enjoys his work, hard though it is, but he is forced by economic circumstances (and by his big brothers) to leave the work he likes, in order to go into the other industries and earn as much as he can during his working life as an actor. Basically this is immoral.

HUGH HUNT:

Would the panel agree that if a choice has to be made between the open stage and the proscenium stage for dramatic performances, then the open stage theatre should be given preference?

PERCY CORRY:

The question is far too vague. There are several forms of open stage. Suppose we imagine that we have sufficient money to build a theatre of our own, and we must be prepared to run it, efficiently and profitably, which form would we build? Well, I would not plump for theatre in the round, and I would not plump for a three-sided stage as at Chichester. I would plump for the open end-stage, which could, if necessary, be transformed quite easily and simply (by fitting adjustable screens) into a proscenium stage. Thereby I would get the best of both worlds. In my opinion that is the only probable successor to the present proscenium stage.

STEPHEN JOSEPH:

This is a sort of a *Desert Island Disc* question. It is very artificial. All of us here, I am sure, feel that every form of theatre is valid. But if you put me on the spot and say 'You have got to have only one!' the answer is, of course, to choose that form of theatre which is going to cater not only for today's audiences but also for tomorrow's, and this, I guess, is the theatre in the round. The proscenium theatre has served its turn. It has evolved into moving pictures and television. If living actors, in front of a living audience, mean anything at all, the one form of theatre that can bring this relationship to a high degree of excitement is the theatre in the round.

CHRISTOPHER STEVENS:

I don't think you can come down and say that one should build one form or another. It depends enormously on who is going to work in your theatre, and how much money you have got. With the sort of money you are likely to have (without subsidy) you will probably get further, have better productions and pay your actors more, if you have a theatre in the round or a stage like Chichester's. There is a snag at Chichester. You spend far more on costumes than anybody ever did behind a proscenium.

DAVID SCASE:

I get the feeling that history has been reversed slightly. If in fact we had had the open stage for the last hundred years both Stephen Joseph and I would be saying 'For goodness' sake let's get behind the pros!' Change is the important thing. But surely you have to consider the play in question? I don't know a great deal about the Questors' plans in Ealing, but there seems to be a design here incorporating successfully three possible forms of presentation—end-stage, the round, and the arena theatre; thus giving one the freedom to decide which form was best suited for a particular play.

STEPHEN JOSEPH:

Obviously it is a most important aspect of art that it moves forward with the times, and, as you say, it is a *change* that we want now. One of the reasons that 500 theatres have closed down in the last 50 years, in this country, is that the conventions of performing behind a hole in the wall are so stale that they are meaningless to the great public.

PERCY CORRY:

Nonsense! The real reason is that the theatre originally provided mass entertainment, but with the introduction of the films, they lost a tremendous amount of appeal, and with the introduction of T.V., both the cinema and the theatre have lost most of their appeal to the masses. There is no reason why the theatre should attempt to imitate the cinema or T.V. The theatre is a perfectly separate and distinct art, and the main difference is, of course, that in the theatre you have a fixed scale and a fixed viewpoint, whereas in the other two media you can vary the scale and the viewpoint as much as you like. And all these appeals against the so-called restrictions of the proscenium stage are nonsense. If an author cannot write for a proscenium stage, or a producer cannot produce on a proscenium stage, he should get out and go into the other media.

W. A. DARLINGTON:

Speaking purely as a playgoer, I want to see every play as near as possible in the conditions for which it is written. And therefore, because the proscenium stage can't be transmogrified into an open stage, while an open stage can be made to fit proscenium methods, I plump for the open stage on this question.

GRENFELL BAINES:

I like the suggestion that you should be able to adapt. These days, architects have to find solutions to enable spaces to be adapted to give flexible use. You simply can't create special spaces for everything. We have heard from the voice of authority that a proscenium stage itself cannot be adapted, and when you think of the solid building required for a proscenium stage with its fire curtain and so on, I can readily believe it. But can an open stage be adapted? You must get audience/actor relationships of different kinds with each different variation. And there is no doubt that a truly adaptable theatre, with an adaptable stage, is also going to have to make provision in some way for adaptable audiences—for adaptable seating. We can't afford extreme mechanical means, but what you can't do with electricity might be done with enthusiasm—and students might shift the seats round, as an exercise in learning about theatre. So I am all for answering this question with the open stage if you can make it adaptable. Let me disclose my interest, finally; I am one of these chaps that have been terribly excited on the other side, the audience side, of the proscenium. And I have still to be converted to the open stage. I have gone a long way tonight but we have got to make it work both ways. I shall believe it possible when I see it.

DAVID SCASE:

I would like to answer Stephen Joseph's accusation, of a few moments back. Let me make it quite clear first, that there is no quarrel between Percy Corry and myself about the idea of a flexible theatre. Most of us have worked in theatre in the round, we have worked on the proscenium stage and we have worked in the horseshoe. Now, this is what I would like to ask you: five or six years ago the theatre was full of excitement over a group of authors. Osborne, Delaney and Brendan Behan, to name a few. One sensed no limitation of enjoyment in the audience when these three authors first hit the scene. But these authors have not produced a second wave of this power, which was to be expected after their first outpourings. Now was it the lack of flexible theatres that prevented these men from developing their talents? Or was it the lack of something that had to be said about the society in which we live? By producing all sorts of flexible theatres; are we going to inspire authors to write new things? Or are they like cornplasters on a wound? Is it that we as people, as a culture, have no dynamic in which to say anything? I am convinced that if we were a country like Israel, or the Russia of say ten years ago, with a social purpose, we would write. And there would be no quarrel with people who say 'Yes, build all kinds of theatres; let's experiment!' But the moment you assume that building a number of different kinds of theatres is going to release the floodgates of writing once again, you fall into a fallacy. When we as a nation have a purpose we can recognize, then we shall have good plays. And you can have theatre anywhere—it is the authors who make it exciting.

STEPHEN JOSEPH:

Differences begin to sharpen between Scase and me. So far Scase has emphasized that the beginning of theatre, or, as it were, the nexus of theatre, is concerned with plays and playwriting. With this I utterly disagree. I think that the experience of theatre is a business between actors and audiences. It is the actors who are the prime movers of the theatre, not the authors.

PERCY CORRY:

The playhouse belongs primarily to the audience. Next it belongs to the author; it is the author who provides the raw material. The actor is a necessity, sometimes a damn nuisance, and not much use unless he has got a first-class director. The entire *avant garde* of the theatre is perplexed, and I think we are doing a great disservice to the theatre by arguing about all these various different forms, each of us damning any other form than the one we favour. The fact is that all forms are permissible and what really matters is: is the play a good one, is the acting good, is the production good in its particular medium and is the presentation good as a whole? It can be presented on any form of stage. But if you are going to advocate a specific form like the promontory stage, or theatre in the round, all the people in the theatre have then got to adjust their tactics and their techniques, and you can't do that lightly, in a minute. If you are going to have a civic theatre you must be extremely careful and not fall into one of these particular traps. If the civic theatre of the future is to be any good at all it must be a theatre which will accept tours from a National Theatre. A civic theatre must be able to present a variety of plays. On the question of adaptability, there are limitations. You can't afford to mess about with the seats. But you can adapt an end-stage, and make it into a proscenium stage if you want to.

HUGH HUNT:

I would like to say that I hope a civic theatre's function will not be merely to receive tours from the National Theatre, but that it will produce plays in the city to which it belongs and produce plays that originate from it. The National Theatre is, as far as I can see, going to belong almost exclusively to the metropolis.

May I go back to the question again? If a choice has to be made between the open stage and the proscenium stage, my advice to any civic authority would be that they should first get themselves a good director. He is the man who must answer this question.

Now the next question is a more personal one:

The Chichester Theatre made use of elements of scenery in each of its three productions this year. Was the theatre planned to cope with problems of changing the scenery, and of storage? Is some illusionist element desirable on this type of stage?

CHRISTOPHER STEVENS:

At the beginning, we certainly didn't expect scenery. I think it would have been very much more difficult to get firemen, the local authority, the police even—all of whom have to make recommendations to the Licensing Magistrates—to agree to the plans if they had known there was going to be so much scenery. If we had had to have a safety curtain and all the space and equipment necessary to handle full-scale scenery, we couldn't have done it without a lot more money and I don't believe the Trustees would have thought they could have raised it.

We always did expect props—probably some pretty big ones even—and some sort of permanent set that maybe could be changed from season to season. I suppose after that it becomes a question of where you can draw the line—painting the set a new colour? changing it between plays? the decision is completely up to the director and what he can persuade people is possible. But if you want to learn a lesson as an architect, it is that within a year your building will be used quite differently from what you had expected.

HUGH HUNT:

So in fact the theatre was not planned to cope with the problems of changing scenery?

CHRISTOPHER STEVENS:

It wasn't originally. And last season very makeshift arrangements were made for it. It was always thought that in the future there would be further extensions to the building, that they might incorporate workshops. But you could not honestly say that, to start with, anybody ever expected scenery.

HUGH HUNT:

There is the first answer to the question. Scenery was an unexpected element at the Chichester Theatre, and was brought in at the director's wish. Mr Joseph, would you answer the second half of the question:

Is some illusionist element desirable on this type of stage?

STEPHEN JOSEPH:

I shall answer the question, though I don't understand it. Words such as 'illusion' baffle me. But here is a theatre that would work marvellously with its permanent architectural background. It was, surely, a mistake to have used it scenically.

HUGH HUNT:

Mr Darlington, do you feel this is true? For instance, could *Uncle Vanya* have been produced without a scenic element?

W. A. DARLINGTON:

I don't think it could. I went to *Uncle Vanya* with one problem in my mind; is the arena stage capable of presenting interior scenes so that they can give the intimacy of the scenic stage? Well, there was that house-front, which seemed to me a very simple form of scenery, and there was certain garden furniture in front of it. At the interval a lighting change, and no other change at all, took 'place; and the house-front became the inside of the house, and the light softened. It had been rustic garden stuff, and suddenly, owing to the softening of the light, it took on almost the look of upholstered furniture. But if the house-front had not been there, I don't think the effect would have been got at all.

HUGH HUNT:

The next question is related to this:

To what extent can lighting be considered a substitute for scenery in creating atmosphere and illusion?

PERCY CORRY:

Lighting can contribute very considerably. But, if I may refer again to *Uncle Vanya*, which I saw, I don't think that the background produced by Sean Kenny contributed anything valuable to the presentation. If you are going to present *Uncle Vanya* on an open stage you must accept the conventions of the open stage. You may use whatever properties are essential to the action. The audience will fill in the blanks. Actually, I thought the effect of shining light through the windows when it was interior and not shining through when it was exterior, didn't really amount to anything at all. It was aggravated by the fact that they didn't light the exits through the doorway. But on the general question of lighting, yes, lighting itself can contribute very considerably. You can't light in a vacuum; you've got to light something. So you must decide whether or not you can dispense with suggestive scenery, or representational scenery, or scenery of any description, and allow the audience to imagine what the setting should be; and by sensitive lighting you can then help the creation of that imaginative concept. Lighting alone has its limitations. On the open stage it is extremely difficult to light isolated areas because of the need to light from all angles.

HUGH HUNT:

This question is confined to Chichester, and not many people have been there; may I ask to what extent lighting might be considered a substitute for scenery in creating illusion?

GRENFELL BAINES:

On this question, I personally love illusion. To be disillusioned seems to be part of my everyday life, and so I like to go to the theatre for its illusion. We seem to be moving into an age of experiment, and we may have to be tested to destruction in this process, without some of the aids we've become accustomed to through the proscenium and so on; and it is far too early, at the moment, to say anything other than 'That's an experiment. Let's try these things.' People may discover, it has been suggested, that their own powers of imagination can produce far more effective illusion than the many artificial aids.

PERCY CORRY:

If they are effectively assisted.

CHRISTOPHER STEVENS:

Both these questions have been thrown at Chichester, as if they only really applied there. I think they apply in every kind of theatre, whether it's behind the proscenium or in front of it. Some people here probably went to Cambridge when the Festival Theatre was working; I didn't, but from what I've seen and read most of these lessons could have been learnt there.

DAVID SCASE:

It is interesting to bring up, at this point, if only briefly, that Brecht found that the use of cross-lighting could be used to create the most wonderful effects to supplement scenery. But he got so sick of this that he asked us to abolish it and actually said: 'Let them dream in blazing light! Don't allow them all to sleep with your lovely night effect.' His demand of the actors was that *they* should create the atmosphere that is inherent in a scene, by the movements of the body, by the handling of props, by their whole behaviour; actors in blazing light can create the atmosphere of night. Brecht asked for the abolition of light used emotionally—let the actor do it, but let the audience see exactly what is happening.

HUGH HUNT:

Now, the next question is quoted from the *Guardian*:

'When it goes well theatre in the round is more engrossing than proscenium arch theatre.' *To what extent does the panel think this is true?*

STEPHEN JOSEPH:

I am very grateful for the comment, but I don't think in fact it is true at the present time. In many of the performances I have seen in theatre in the round (some of which I have produced myself, such as last night's) there is always a large section of the audience so strange to the idea of theatre in the round that they are continually aware of odd things, of seeing the audience opposite, of the actors' backs. They look round to see how the stage is lit, they observe the way a fairly unsuitable hall has been adapted. I would like to think that ordinary people and critics alike were mature enough to rise above these things, but I am afraid it just isn't so. I look forward to going to an innocent place, such as Scarborough, where most people who come to the theatre are not theatre-goers. They are much more willing to accept theatre in the round, and because they are innocent they do seem to get a very much greater excitement from it than they would from ordinary proscenium production; but I don't think this is general.

W. A. DARLINGTON:

I haven't a very great experience of theatre in the round. I saw the *Glass Menagerie* at Oxford, and I felt it a bit disconcerting to find myself sitting beside the household garbage can. I couldn't adjust myself to the fact that the garbage can was in the play and I was not. Also I found it disconcerting at the Pembroke Theatre, Croydon, when people were being murdered or raped right under my nose, and among my feet. I'm not really a very good witness on the point because so far I haven't been persuaded.

PERCY CORRY:

I have seen a number of theatre in the round performances, some good, some bad, some unbearable. I share Mr Darlington's feelings; when a young lady is breathing heavily, perspiring on the top lip, and emoting violently within about three feet of me, I find it a bit disconcerting. But nonetheless in a production that is well done, well acted, a good play can be just as moving in theatre in the round, just as absorbing in theatre in the round, as it can be on proscenium stage. There are decided possibilities. There are difficulties; and you have to adjust the technique to suit the medium. I wouldn't say theatre in the round is better, I wouldn't say that it is generally worse; for me it has certain disadvantages which make me prefer the end-stage.

DAVID SCASE:

I know that most people haven't had ladies raped between their feet. However, most of us have sat next to garbage cans, and most of us have observed perspiration at fairly close quarters. The cinema would go all out to try and create a sense of the proximity of perspiration, or of rape, or of garbage cans, to make us feel right on top of these events; but somehow one remains detached and can watch this without embarrassment. But when you achieve this in the theatre, and have real proximity it does provoke in many people a sense of embarrassment. I don't know why this is so. I must say, however, in answer to the question, that when I have seen theatre in the round at its best, it has produced more excitement in the audience, particularly in the twenty minutes after leaving the theatre (which is the important time) than the proscenium theatre at its best. But I think Stephen Joseph would say that at the Pembroke Theatre the relationship between audience and stage was appalling. No one should be asked to sit actually on top of the garbage cans! Theatre in the round doesn't mean that we have to be breathing down each others necks. There should be a moat, if you like, a psychological moat, which allows the actor to be close with just that gap between. I went to several performances of *Hay Fever*, of all plays one you would think was a proscenium arch play, and it was done on a stage where the audience sat two-thirds of the way round. Over and over again people coming out said that never before had they felt that they were part and parcel of that party going on in that house. This didn't create embarrassment. It was real contact between actors and their audience.

HUGH HUNT:

The answer to this question really hangs on the fact that no theatre in the round has been adequately built up to now in this country.

GRENFELL BAINES:

Someone who saw the performance in the round the other night said that their first impression was that they had never seen so many chilblains and corns. So they, too, must have been embarrassed by this proximity.

STEPHEN JOSEPH:

We tend to criticize or comment on certain aspects of theatre in the round: you see the actors' chilblains. But I went recently to the Royal Court Theatre (which is a very conventional theatre) to see Rex Harrison play in *August for the People*. He had green eyelids. I thought it was the whole point of the play that the character was diseased. But the object of the green eyelids and, indeed, all the make-up, was simply to convince people at the back of the theatre that the actor had a face.

HUGH HUNT:

The next question is about the amateur theatre:

Most amateur theatres today are built in the proscenium pattern. Does the Brains Trust consider that amateurs should experiment in new forms, or is experimentation only valid in the hands of experts?

PERCY CORRY:

No, I don't think experiment is only valid with the experts. But curiously enough the amateur theatre is way behind the professional theatre in this readiness to experiment today. It wasn't in the past. At the beginning of this century it was the amateur theatre that led the field of experiment to a large

A A A—H

extent. Amateurs tend to stick to the proscenium stage because it is the theatre they know. Let us be quite clear about why the amateur theatre has grown to such an extent. With the decline of the professional theatre after the onslaught of films, and subsequently television, hundreds of places were left without any theatre whatever. So people proceeded to make their own. It is estimated that there are something like 30,000 amateur societies in this country, all regularly producing plays; with varying degrees of ability. But the point is that they got make-shift theatres, of the sort that they knew, with the proscenium arch. But there are quite a number of theatres trying to break away. The notable example, of course, is the Questors at Ealing who are making an extraordinary experiment with an adaptable theatre with a view, if possible, to resolving this vexed problem of which is the best form for contemporary theatre.

W. A. DARLINGTON:

It's a small point, but most of the 30,000 amateur societies are not in a position to experiment even if they want to.

HUGH HUNT:

Yes, I think it is true to say that early in the century the amateur movement was very experimental. There was the Maddermarket Theatre, Stockport Garrick, Barry Jackson's theatre; but it has lost the leadership in experiment today. There is no reason why it shouldn't regain it.

Now the next question applies to the Chichester Theatre, but we won't confine it:

There was some criticism of the acoustics of the Chichester Theatre. How far is this due to the construction and how far to the fact that modern actors have disregarded the art of dramatic speech?

CHRISTOPHER STEVENS:

One probably could improve the acoustics. It is very difficult to know what a building will really do until you have an audience in it, and can try it. If there are any weaknesses at Chichester, in mitigation there is one point I would put forward; we didn't have a lot of money. This lecture room is full of stuff which is here purely for acoustic purposes. There isn't anything at Chichester like that; each material has to do something else as well. It either keeps the rain out, or makes a wall; everything had to have two purposes to get in there at all. We couldn't afford to build the theatre over-large and leave room for a lot of adjustment. It is as small as one dared make it. The volume is important in acoustics. We didn't even know, when we had to decide how big and what shape the building was, whether the audience were going to sit on concrete or on upholstered chairs. There wasn't carpet until the last couple of months before it opened. All those considerations go to make a lot of difference and, honestly, I don't think one can be surprised that we do need some adjustments.

HUGH HUNT:

May we pass to the second part of the question:

The fact that modern actors have disregarded the art of dramatic speech.

W. A. DARLINGTON:

I feel that this is extremely true. I have been suffering from inaudible actors for many years. Lilian Braithwaite at a meeting of the Critics' Circle, just after the War, towards the end of her life, got up and implored us as a body of critics to go for the actors who were absolutely falling below any standard which she could recognize as being professionally adequate. And I started a one-man crusade. After a bit a producer called Reginald Tate, who was a friend of mine, met me in the street and said, 'Keep this up. Because I heard the other day of a producer who got his company together at the beginning of rehearsals and said, "Now, boys and girls, this is a modern play, so don't let's be too dreadfully audible." ' May I go on to Chichester? As one who saw all three productions at Chichester, I should like to suggest that the objections against the acoustics there were not so much that actors do not speak up, because nearly all of the company were pretty good speakers. But I did find that, seated as I was in the middle of the front of that very wide stage, that when somebody was at the extreme other end of it, with his back to me and talking to the audience out on the flank of the arena stage, he was inaudible simply because nobody could have been audible under the circumstances—unless he yelled. Even one of the best speakers in the world on the stage, Laurence Olivier, was inaudible for a considerable part of one of the plays. The only person who was fully audible in *Uncle Vanya* was Sybil Thorndike, because she sat in the middle of the stage, facing the main part of the audience, and she had the whole audience under her vocal control, so to speak; but the people who had to go out and act on the flanks of that enormous stage could not be heard by the people who were furthest away. I think the distances on that stage were larger between some of the audience and some of the actors than has ever happened in a theatre in my experience before.

HUGH HUNT:

Could we pick up the theme that actors have lost the art of dramatic speech, or disregarded it? Now, David Scase, you deal with a small theatre where problems of acoustics are not so great. Would you say that you encourage your actors to be inaudible, or would you encourage the art of projection? And to what extent can a psychological play, of our own day, be projected in a large theatre?

DAVID SCASE:

I think the critics who say that we shout in the theatre are partly to blame for this inaudibility. Most of the actors in our company have actors' voices. This is the first thing we look for. It is quite true that a number of actors who come to auditions have not got voices. It is frightening how many come each year from drama schools and appear to have had no vocal training whatsoever. It is a fallacy to think the Library Theatre, Manchester, is a small theatre vocally. You have to use as much voice in the Library Theatre as in the Opera House. The whole art of projection is to able to project even a modern psychological play, which apparently has moments of quietness, so that anyone in the theatre can receive that moment of quietness and think of it as such; or, when there is a moment of greatness or bigness, to be able to use the voice in a big way, which does not deafen the audience, but creates a sense that a man is roaring his heart out at this moment. May I go back to the open stage and quote John English? He has said that here we all have to learn to use a much bigger voice, and a different technique. You have to build the voice; this can be done. There is no problem of audibility with good voices in theatre in the round or on the open stage.

HUGH HUNT:

You have suggested that it is a problem of training for different forms of theatre. And probably this is not being undertaken by the dramatic schools at the present time. Is it also true that dramatic schools are, in some cases, not training actors to speak clearly and to throw their voices?

STEPHEN JOSEPH:

I'm not sure that it is fair to blame the drama schools. Some of them, certainly, try to give their students a good, systematic course in speech training. I would like to put the blame on architects. Too many buildings in this country are built, by tradition, in a way unsuited to their function. Public halls, in particular, have been built to imitate Egyptian tombs, Greek temples, Roman baths or Arabian mausoleums. Of course, they are acoustically inadequate. Nowadays a gesture may be made towards the science of acoustics—but only a gesture. Acoustics is treated like a black art. There are all sorts of magical words and mixtures, and pins stuck into the wax images of actors. The result is usually bad acoustics. In America it is much easier, of course. They have halls and theatres with open stages where actors can easily be heard. But acoustic problems are not the same for them. I believe it has something to do with the weather, or central heating, or, perhaps, their actors. Perhaps they audition their actors before casting them, whereas we tend to cast, in this country, over the dinner table in a smart restaurant. It is an honoured custom.

DAVID SCASE:

But I must question what Stephen Joseph says about actors. I am sure that in the past no actor has been taken into a company without an audition. But I have met actors recently who have been working in the theatre for some two or three years, who were amazed when asked to audition. They have never been auditioned. They have been spoken to, quietly, over a glass of beer in a pub or in an office. Well, how on earth can you tell what a person is like in the office, unless you at least ask them to go on stage to hear what their voices are like?

GRENFELL BAINES:

It is not really true that acoustics are different in America from here. A lot of work has been done here in this country. In fact, I think we are pioneers of how to arrange a building in order to help distribute sound properly. I also want to make a new point; in an adaptable theatre, where you may have a proscenium or an open stage, the relationship of the audience to the speakers is quite important to the way sound is distributed. Here is where the smaller theatre will undoubtedly score, because the sound comes direct instead of being reflected. There is no doubt about it that the services that are appropriate when people are speaking from a stage with a proscenium are not always appropriate when they are outside. What should absorb in one case, must reflect once you have reversed the conditions. This is one of those nice things that we are going to have to tackle in due course.

HUGH HUNT:

We are coming to the end of the evening. I'm going to ask two more questions:

If theatre is to revive in the battle of the audiences, against television and cinema, what steps do you think the theatre should take to meet this competition?

DAVID SCASE:

I don't know. After all, it is a fight that has been going on for some time now. We were more terrified about it five years ago, when the full impact of television came to the entire country, when we were first networked both by the B.B.C. and by I.T.V. We have reached that point now where most people, in a city like Manchester, who want television can have it, and they are making their choice now between television and theatre. Most of the weekly reps had an enormous battle to fight to maintain any kind of standard and they fell before television. Other companies that had a chance of maintaining a standard, with three or four weeks' rehearsal, tried not to compete but to show the difference between television and theatre and cinema. For they are totally different media. Perhaps, then, there is no fight. People of my age mainly put their feet up before television. I do regularly. We are perfectly satisfied to stay at home. But young people today are much more critical. They are not seduced by television. These are the people who go out. And they want to go to the theatre. They like the sense of occasion and of social concord that exist in the theatre at its best. They do not want to sit at home with the telly, constantly interrupted by cups of tea, and dogs, and kids and so on. But millions of people are seeing drama on television who have never been near a theatre in their lives. They see Ibsen, Shakespeare, Arthur Miller and even Terence Rattigan. If they are once seduced into saying, 'There is a play, by the same man we saw on telly last week, down at the theatre', and they come into the theatre, we could win a wonderful new audience. I am quite convinced that if people come from television to theatre at its best, there is no competition. They will stay with us, if we are good when they come.

GRENFELL BAINES:

Isn't that exactly what has happened with radio and music? Our concert halls are full of young people because of the music that radio brought. When I was a boy, to hear a decent work of music was a miracle in our town. When radio came we began to hear it. And then we began to go to the concert hall. We even went from Preston to Manchester. And this is what will happen with the theatre. But as an ordinary theatre-goer, may I say that I think you will compete best by being just sufficiently intriguing without baffling; in other words, be good and let who will be clever.

PERCY CORRY:

There are several things that theatre could do. In the first place, we must provide pleasing and comfortable conditions for the playgoer. Most of the theatres in this country, except a few new ones, are penitential. You know, Shaw said that the Englishman thinks he is being moral when he's only uncomfortable; there's a lot in that. And I think we have to provide congenial surroundings and make visiting the theatre a social occasion. We must also get rid of this idea that the public has a duty to support the theatre; that people must be imbued with a religious fervour for the theatre, and that, if they don't support the theatre, they are in some way decadent. The theatre must impinge on the public so that they want to come and see it. And that brings us really to the crux of it, doesn't it? We've got to have great dramatists, we've got to have efficient, competent actors (who can be heard), we've got to have interesting and exciting presentation. With these things, I am quite certain that we can get a sufficient percentage of the population to keep the theatre not only alive, but kicking.

STEPHEN JOSEPH:

I agree with most of what has been said, but I want to add, very strongly, that I believe the actor/audience relationship must be examined, and explored. We have talked about it several times this evening. The thing that happens in the living theatre is a co-operative creation between actors and audience. And the most powerful way of achieving this is by spreading the audience round the acting area, and close to it.

DAVID SCASE:

I agree. And it is surely true that the open stage is coming in.

HUGH HUNT:

I think the panel feels that besides having first-class acting, and besides having first-class plays and creating an atmosphere that is more inviting in the theatre, the theatre itself has got to renew its architectural form. This may be achieved through the proscenium theatre, through the open-stage theatre, the theatre in the round, or through an adaptable theatre, but at all events the theatre must try to meet the new audiences that are coming from—and can yet come from—television. We don't feel that television or the cinema are rivals to the theatre; they can be propagandist agents for it. But if the theatre is to absorb the new audiences then it must provide a new sense of excitement. This cannot be achieved by the actor or the artist alone; they must have the co-operation of the architect.

Now I'm going to throw one more question at the panel before we finish:

Why should the theatre survive? What makes theatre people so self-important?

W. A. DARLINGTON:

At the age of nine I went to the theatre for the first time, and I just fell in love with it. I've been in love with it ever since. I can't explain that, it just happened to me.

GRENFELL BAINES:

One of the difficulties in life today is to hold on to values that have been established. Things are happening so swiftly. People go into new things and new adventures, and we have seen a lot of throwing away things that were really good. We pursue things that seem to offer a change for the sake of change. Theatre has been one of the permanent things in civilization, and it has contributed enormously to the architecture of our cities. Some of the really grand baroque theatres are still worth looking at. Of course theatre should survive. It is an emblem of a civilized society.

CHRISTOPHER STEVENS:

I want theatre to survive. I enjoy reading books, I like going to the cinema; I also like going to the theatre. And I go to the theatre for a different reason, and I get something quite different from it. It might perhaps do better if theatre people (and architects) were not quite so filled with their own importance, and if we could make it a little more commonplace, a little less magical. I don't mean that I want it to be popular, because 'popular' tends to mean spending a lot of money to provide something that everybody can go and see without being allowed to think; and I hate going to the theatre for plays that I don't have to think about.

DAVID SCASE:

I don't think you can stop theatre. Its funeral dirge has been going on for centuries, and it has lasted as long as civilization. I've already said that it reflects the health of any nation at a given time. It is not for us to make it survive. Society will do this. If there is any self-importance, you cannot entirely blame theatre people for it; it is partly a product of press and public relations.

HUGH HUNT:

Mr Darlington, you're partly responsible then for making theatre people self-important. Why do you feel the theatre should survive?

W. A. DARLINGTON:

Well, to me it is rather like the question 'Why did you marry your wife?' It has never occurred to me at any time that the theatre should not survive, nor that there would be anybody who would think it should not survive. It is, to me, a fundamental part of civilization for which no mechanical kind of thing can make up. I am perfectly happy at the cinema and I have once seen a television play; I fell asleep in the middle of it. I'm an inveterate reader, but the theatre gives me something of its own, which I value. I should have to have notice of the question if I wanted to analyse quite what that is, but it is completely sufficient to me and therefore it is important to me. Whether it is self-important is something which I don't really understand.

PERCY CORRY:

It must survive. You can't prevent it from surviving because it represents a relationship which is basic between people. It is true that, in this century, we have never treated the theatre as an essential part of the cultural life of the community, but we are moving towards that. The theatre has always existed in some form and it always will exist.

STEPHEN JOSEPH:

I think we have all been a little complacent about this question. With the tremendous strides made by television, there is, in spite of our general feeling that television can help the theatre, a movement by people away from the theatre. What the question is asking us is surely 'What is theatre for?' If we can recognize what theatre is for, we may also explain our own feelings of importance. Theatre doesn't begin with one group of people—writers, actors, or directors—who offer something to the audience. Theatre begins, in almost every civilization, with the joint demand—the audience want actors every bit as much as actors want an audience. The phenomenon of the theatre is simply this, that there should be a huge celebration, communally done by audience and actors alike; it says 'Hurray, we are human beings! We can do things. We have control over our destiny. Life is exciting! Life is beautiful! Good!' The actors show it, the audience say 'We agree' and applaud. Actors have some justification for feeling that they are important, because they are the great priests of life.

HUGH HUNT:

Actors did start as the great priests of life, and if they have now fallen below this status then perhaps there may be a turning point and the actors of the future will again occupy the same important part in life that they did in earlier days. This turning point will be reflected in the type and standard of theatre building which the architect is called upon to build. It may well be that we have at last reached this turning point. If so, the architect, as well as the actor, has a vital part to play.

Index

Titles of plays are given in italics

117